That The World May Know

Earl Paulk

Copyright 1987
K Dimension Publishers
Atlanta, Georgia

Printed in the United States of America
ISBN 0-917595-15-7

P.O. Box 7300 • Atlanta, GA 30357

DEDICATION

Dr. David J. du Plessis

In an extraordinary ministry spanning six decades, Dr. David J. du Plessis, "Mr. Pentecost," has embodied the ecumenical thrust of the renewal movement in the Church. No man since the Apostle Paul has shown more tenacity toward bringing unity to the body of Christ than David du Plessis. His bold proclamation and demonstration of Jesus' prayer in John 17 has been the catalyst for breakthroughs in spiritual oneness that few Christians would have ever believed to be possible.

David du Plessis dared to cross dividing lines and knocked down walls separating Christians. He has sailed an uncharted course. As a result of his unique calling, he has known love and rejection, honor and disdain, gratitude and misunderstanding. He has remained a good and faithful servant to the obedience of Christ in what must have seemed at times to be an impossible mission. This servant performed the apostolic miracle of joining obstinate, stiff-necked people to one another in bonds of Christian love. And through this servant, God has opened doors that no man can shut.

In January 1983, Dr. du Plessis called Bishop John Meares and me into his hotel room at the conclusion of the evening session of the Idea Exchange, an annual conference of pastors sharing ministry concerns which was held that year in Orlando, Florida. Several members of my staff accompanied us to Dr. du Plessis' room as witnesses to what unquestionably has become a milestone in both John Meares' and my ministries.

Dr. du Plessis simply defined his calling and shared with us the mandate that God had entrusted to him. Speaking from the undeniable loneliness of a visionary, he sensed that John Meares and I would understand. How well we understood. John is the white pastor of a predominantly black congregation at the great church, Evangel Temple, in the inner city of Washington, D.C. I minister to an innovative church with a racially mixed congregation in Atlanta, Georgia, at the heart of Bible-belt traditions and racial and religious prejudices. Yes, we understood the privilege and burden of the cross David du Plessis carried.

Then Dr. du Plessis said that he wanted to pray over us. In timeless, eternal words of spiritual impartation, he prayed that his mantle would fall upon Bishop John Meares and me. He exhorted us to carry on the work he had begun to bring unity to the body of Christ. I remember wondering at the time whether

iv

he felt his course was almost complete.

We repeatedly contemplate spiritually significant incidents during the storms and triumphs of life. The mystery of David du Plessis' prayer continually unfolds in my spirit. The message of unity burns like fire within me. Instead of protecting myself from the struggles that the gospel of peace inevitably ignite in satanic forces, I run headlong into the battle with a bold proclamation. Repeatedly, I feel the sting of misunderstanding, but also the unspeakable joy of doors opening by the keys of the Kingdom of God as His truth storms the gates of hell.

David du Plessis lies awaiting his homegoing as this book goes to press. He has called his wife, Anna, and his family around him, and according to his brother, Justus, his room is filled with the peace of God. Peace rests upon faithful warriors who have fought the good fight. I honor David du Plessis' message and vision, but I also give honor to the obedient vessel!

To whatever measure God directs my ministry in His sovereignty and will in the days ahead, I receive David du Plessis' mantle and wear it with gratitude and joy. Both John Meares and I press toward fulfilling the prayer of our brother's bold exhortation, spoken by the power of the Holy Spirit. And I pray that this book, dedicated to David du Plessis, will hasten the fulfillment of Jesus' prayer in John 17 for the unity of His beloved Church.

Bishop Earl Paulk

ACKNOWLEDGEMENTS

I wish to thank the Publications Department of Chapel Hill Harvester Church for their daily efforts and continuing dedication to the Lord in the preparation of this book.

I thank my Editorial Assistant, Tricia Weeks, for her capable contribution in writing and editing.

I deeply appreciate the proficiency of our Editorial Staff—Gayle Blackwood and Chris Oborne.

I thank Wes Bonner for his expertise in coordinating the technical aspects of publishing this book. I also give special thanks to Nancy Dugger for editing and typesetting.

Finally, I am especially grateful for the volunteers who gave their time and skills to further the message of the Kingdom of God: Angela Hamrick and Linda Jacobson for transcribing, and Janis McFarland for proofreading.

May the seeds of these words bear much fruit for the glory of the Kingdom of God.

The importance of the book you are about to read cannot be overstated. At a time when the Spirit of God is literally crying out within the Body of Christ for unity and fellowship, Bishop Earl Paulk has stepped forward to give us a true New Testament foundation. Since unity is the key to God's commanded blessing, there would no doubt be those who (in the name of Christ) would be manipulated to stand against God's manifested purpose in the Church.

Whether these opposers are malicious in their attempts to fragment the Church is for God to judge. The bottom line on their faulty exegesis is revealed in the fruit and overall effect of their warring spirits. That fruit is division and therein destructive.

Earl Paulk delicately dissects those who have been deceived. He reveals the true nature of "the counterfeit" versus "the real" in the context of the true New Testament gospel. Without skirting the accusation that those who are "unity men are wolves cloaked in the New Age" garments, Earl Paulk courageously shows the contrast between the gospel of the Kingdom of God and the unholy deception which denies the Lord Who bought them.

The heart of this book calls us to become whom Christ created us to be. We are truly becoming the head and not the tail. Take this book and read it prayerfully and you will find a new vision come forth for your future and the future of the Church.

Someone had to write this book. I was thrilled when I read it knowing that your life will be changed as you do the same.

Prayerfully,

Dr. Larry Lea
Church on the Rock
Rockwall, Texas

INTRODUCTION

Evangelical Christians, regardless of their denominations or traditions, agree that something significant is happening in Church history in our generation. All of us feel the deep rumblings which cause spiritual shaking. We hear reverberating, "The cloud of God is moving! The trumpet is sounding!" Numerous contemporary examples demonstrate that those words are becoming far more than biblical imagery in the lives of Christians around the world. The "sleeping giant" of the Church is waking up and speaking up with new power and authority.

Consequently, Christian literature of such a time as this reflects the dynamics of motion and sound. Shaking is never comfortable. Many people resist change—even when God initiates it. The deluge of writers explaining, promoting or objecting to the spiritual significance of our day only contributes to its prophetic validity. Indeed, Jesus said that deception would characterize the last days. If possible, even the very elect could listen to the wrong people and follow the wrong directions.

Dave Hunt's and T.A. McMahon's *Seduction of Christianity* has adequately pressed certain issues to the forefront of Christian dialogue. As a researcher on the occult, Mr. Hunt warns Christians to exercise caution in openly accepting "new" teaching, promises, miracles, or doctrines that probe man's inner being. He writes about the cults he has studied, and explains the dangers of occult beliefs infiltrating Christianity. His concerns become personalized by the ministers he calls into question. He quotes Paul Yonggi Cho, Robert Schuller, Mother Teresa, Bruce Larson, Robert Tilton, Rita Bennet, Charles Capps, Kenneth Copeland, and many others.

As the air begins to clear from emotionally charged reactions to Mr. Hunt's personalized warnings, the need to examine the issues he raises has never been greater. If Dave Hunt is accurate in his assessments of certain ministries he names, the Church needs to bring correction and healing quickly. If Dave Hunt has made errors in his assessments, correction and healing are still vitally necessary. *Seduction of Christianity* does far more than raise questions. The book has brought confusion and division to perhaps the most bold, outspoken branch of the Church in the days which could well become her most glorious.

Because I am quoted in Dave Hunt's book, I have been contacted by several television "talk show" producers to appear with Dave Hunt and discuss our differences publicly. I was willing to participate in such an exchange program as long as the goals of our discussion would be positive in ending the controversy surrounding some of the ministers named in Mr. Hunt's book. God intervened in preventing those broadcasts. Instead, through circumstances I had not anticipated, God allowed for me to meet Dave Hunt in a forum arranged by Evangelist Jimmy Swaggart at his Bible college in Baton Rouge, Louisiana. Details of that meeting, which I share in this book, have convinced me to be even more resolute in pointing out the greater dangers to the Church underlying some of Dave Hunt's warnings.

I believe the Kingdom of God is built in trust. I am alarmed at the suspicion clouding the important issues that God's people need to confront today. As governments crumble in scandal, the world's economy totters and men's hearts fail them for fear, God's people must arise with discernment as the *Daniel's* and *Joseph's* of our day. We need bold, confident leaders who hear God's voice and speak God's direction.

Before you, the reader, consider my perspective on the issues of controversy, you have a right to know my own theological convictions:

• I believe the Bible to be the inspired, the only infallible, authoritative Word of God.

• I believe in only one God, eternally existent in three persons: Father, Son and Holy Spirit.

• I believe in the deity of our Lord Jesus Christ, in His virgin birth, in His sinless life, in His miracles, in His vicarious suffering and atoning death through

His shed blood, in His bodily resurrection, in His ascension to the right hand of the Father, and in His personal return to earth in power and glory.

• I believe that for the salvation of lost and sinful man, regeneration by the Holy Spirit is absolutely essential.

• I believe in the present ministry of the Holy Spirit by whose indwelling the Christian is empowered to live a godly life.

• I believe in the resurrection of both the saved and the lost; of those who are saved to the resurrection of life, and of those who are lost to the resurrection of damnation.

• I believe in the spiritual unity of believers in our Lord Jesus Christ as His body in the world.

I am the pastor of an interdenominational church, Chapel Hill Harvester Church in Atlanta, Georgia. I began my ministry at age seventeen. I graduated from a Baptist college, Furman University, and a Methodist Seminary, Candler School of Theology at Emory University. For eight years I served as the senior pastor of a large church in Atlanta. In 1960 when I was thirty-three years old, God gave me a vision of a church which would become a city of refuge caring for "scattered sheep." The name "Harvester" comes from Matthew 9:37,38, "Then He said to His disciples, 'The harvest truly is plentiful, but the laborers are few. Therefore pray the Lord of the harvest to send out laborers into His harvest.' "

In 1982 I received a vision from God that changed my understanding of God's commission for His Church in the world. Since that time, I have proclaimed the Kingdom of God with an unexplainable urgency which burns like a consuming fire in my spirit. I speak now as a "provoker" to the universal

Church to confront prejudices and traditions which hinder the move of God in His people today. My goal is to bring Christians to spiritual maturity and unity in the knowledge of Jesus Christ. I am dedicated to the healing of the wounded body of Christ.

We comprehend the spiritual realm by life in the natural world. I believe that the tragedy of millions of babies aborted in our generation represents millions of spiritual babies aborted before they reach maturity—the full stature of Christ. When Moses was born, male Hebrew babies were killed because Satan knew that God heard the cry of His people. When Jesus was born in Bethlehem of Judea, Satan moved upon Herod to kill the male Jewish children in an attempt to kill the Deliverer, our Redeemer, the King of the Jews.

Today God hears the cry of His people. A deliverer is growing up in the earth. She is the Church, the bride of Christ. She lives in a hostile environment just as Moses and Jesus did. Satan wants to kill her before she reaches full maturity. Neither our warfare nor our weapons are carnal. Empowered since the day of that heavenly visitation of the Holy Spirit at Pentecost, the Church is becoming a city set on a hill. She is maturing, learning through obedience to know the mind of Christ. She is being sanctified in the righteousness of Christ, without spot or wrinkle, and is becoming a standard by which world systems will be judged.

The maturing process is painful. No one has all the answers. The body of Christ is "fitly joined together," requiring us to need one another. Keen discernment is essential to spiritual maturity. Dialogue is absolutely necessary for us to understand the full counsel of God's voice to us as His Word unfolds in our generation. At times everyone's perspective will need correction and refining. But the enemies of the maturing Church should be warned; the mysteries of God are unfolding. Had Satan understood the mystery of the Incarnation, he would not have crucified the King of glory.

And to those called according to God's purposes in our day, all the strife, controversy, accusations and painful persecution work for our good—abundantly, exceedingly, beyond all we can ask or think!

Our King Cometh!

Earl Paulk, Bishop

TABLE OF CONTENTS

FATHER, MAKE US ONE

I'm really nothing without you.
I need you just to survive.
How can the hand say it has no need
Of the arm, the ear or the eye?
We're so intricately joined together.
Even our blood is the same.
How can we mend a broken world
If his body's ripped and maimed?

Let's stop this fighting each other
And defeat our true enemy.
How can we crush down the gates of hell
Till we march in unity?
The ongoing incarnation of Jesus
Is you and me, the body of Christ.
How can the world see Him lifted up
If we don't lift Him up in our lives?

CHORUS
We really need each other.
Father, make us one
So that the world will know You loved them
So much You gave Your Son.
We really need each other.
Father, make us one
So that the world will know You loved them
So much You gave Your Son.
Father, make us one.
Father, make us one.

BRIDGE
Reach out and take each other's hand
And forgive the hurts of the past.
It's time we stand up . . .
So that the world can see
The hope of Christ in us at last.

A song by Dony McGuire & Reba Rambo McGuire

1

THAT THE WORLD MAY KNOW

I turned from the podium to my left and looked at Evangelist Jimmy Swaggart. I told him that I perceive him to be a covenant brother in Christ and an elder in the universal Church. I recognize his ministry as a called evangelist in whom God has given an opportunity to lead people to salvation in Jesus Christ at a scope granted to few men in any generation.

Then I looked over Jimmy Swaggart's shoulder to address author Dave Hunt who wrote the highly controversial book, *Seduction of Christianity.* I told Mr. Hunt that I regarded him to be a researcher of the occult who has written about areas of contemporary

Christian teaching that the Church must examine. With that commendation, I questioned the reasons that Mr. Hunt began a book of research on occult infiltration by reminding his readers of Jim Jones' shocking tragedy in Jonestown, and then subsequently called into question the ministries of such men of God as Paul Yonggi Cho and Kenneth Copeland.

I traveled to Baton Rouge, Louisiana, to the campus of Jimmy Swaggart Bible College in mid-November 1986. I had requested a meeting with Jimmy Swaggart to give answers to my biblical perspective of the Kingdom of God. The same God Who sent Jonah to Nineveh pressed me to answer the accusations against my teaching raised by Jimmy Swaggart in an article he wrote in the September issue of his monthly publication, *The Evangelist.* According to Matthew 5:23,24, I needed to reconcile with my brother who obviously had an offense against me. I also felt the exhortation to follow the instructions of 1 Peter 3:15 in giving "a defense." This defense was not intended for the world, but to one whom I consider to be my brother in Christ.

Instead of the private meeting I had requested with Jimmy Swaggart, I stood at a podium before approximately forty men and women: members of the college faculty, pastors from the Baton Rouge area, Jimmy Swaggart's wife and son, author Dave Hunt and two Assembly of God pastors whom I regard as elders, Tommy Reid and Quintan Edwards. I was grateful for the opportunity for a hearing, regardless of the meeting format. However, I was unprepared to address an assembly except by the indwelling Holy Spirit in Whom we are ready in and out of season. I had no previous knowledge that Dave Hunt, who

2

quoted me in *Seduction of Christianity,* would be in Baton Rouge on that November afternoon.

I thanked Evangelist Swaggart for the opportunity to speak to such a notable assembly and to meet Dave Hunt. I emphasized that I regarded Mr. Hunt to be a layman, a researcher and an expert on the occult. I felt I must clarify that I do not consider Dave Hunt to be a theologian, nor a man called by God to bring admonishment to ministries. In fact, I asked Dave Hunt if he had come to Baton Rouge under the covering of his own pastor or spiritual leader.

I must admit that I would never have chosen to answer the challenges to my teaching in this setting. I am convinced that controversy in the Church is settled best privately, behind closed doors just as the early Church dealt with their disputes regarding circumcision (Acts 15). By following this scriptural example, Christians may stand as a united front in giving answers to the world. We jeopardize our witness to the gospel of Jesus Christ before an unbelieving society groping in darkness by airing our disputes. How can unsaved people possibly believe that Jesus offers them hope and solutions when they observe Christians fighting each other? On the basis of numbers of people around the U-shaped table in that room, I knew this meeting would produce an assortment of interpretations and conclusions.

Christians have a responsibility as members of the one family of God when we address the world. We of all people must be careful not to condemn our brothers and sisters as the world listens caustically to a Christian's perspective. If anything, we are called to protect the unity of the Church. Jesus' prayer in John 17 calls us to oneness "that the world may believe..."

3

With such a cry from God's heart in intercession for us, how dare we flaunt our differences before the world? Do we so easily forget that Jesus told His disciples that they would be recognized by all men because of their love for one another? (John 13:35). Does "love for one another" distinguish disciples of Jesus today? Jesus promised it would!

An example of our responsibility as protectors of the Church is found in the story of Mary and Joseph's betrothal. Joseph wrestled with grave decisions at receiving the news that his bride-to-be was pregnant. Joseph's dilemma represents the spirit of God's covering. He decided to "put her (Mary) away privately" to protect her. Symbolically, this story represents the covering of the Church during growth and maturity, being tossed to and fro until the "fullness of time." Of course our faults are obvious to one another as we grow to maturity, but the Bible teaches that "love covers."

Our responsibility to the world is to preach the gospel of the Kingdom. Jesus did not come to condemn the world, but that the world through Him might be saved. That message is the gospel or "good news." If Christians are to judge angels one day, the world must view us as a community of love for one another with a gospel of hope—not as a community torn in disputes and fragmented in our differences. Too many Christians are unwilling to be reconciled. Where is the hope in such dissension? Where is the love identifying disciples of Christ? What sign distinguishes us from the rest of the world?

Such covering is not characteristic of the content of *Seduction of Christianity,* nor of articles addressing Kingdom teaching written by Evangelist Jimmy Swaggart. A message of hope and restoration of the glorious Church is not the theme of Hal Lindsey's apocalyptic predictions in *The Late, Great Planet Earth*. Christians are given few reasons for rejoicing at the future of the Church by reading David Wilkerson's *The Vision*. These messages are condemnations of the Church as a failing institution, written to a world responding in dismay at hearing our differences and pessimistic predictions. The purported themes of these writers offer little, if any, good news.

Of course some will respond that the prophets of old cried out "doom" against Israel. But notice that these prophesies were warnings **against Israel** who had forgotten her covenant with God. Old Testament prophets spoke warnings against mixture and spiritual adultery to a nation chosen by God to reveal His Son. After Jesus' resurrection, He gave the fivefold ministry to bring His body into unity and maturity (Ephesians 4). Prophets called by God today are birthed out of the loins of Christ. They are prophets in the spirit of Melchizedek, prophets of hope and covenant, reconciling men to God through restoration. Jesus' first sermon, reading from Isaiah 61, proclaimed good news to the poor, healing to the brokenhearted, deliverance to captives, sight to the blind, liberty to those who were oppressed, and the acceptable year of the Lord (Luke 4:18,19). Now that's good news!

God's Word gives clear instructions on how to settle disputes among believers. Imagine the variety of perspectives, experiences and motivations even among the disciples who walked with Jesus. In the early Church we have writings from a doctor, a fisherman, a tax collector. In their obvious differences they were one through a common focus. They were all followers of Jesus. Of the twelve Jesus chose,

5

only one broke his covenant relationship with Christ, and that finality came by Judas' committing suicide. Covenant with Christ is far more binding than our comprehension of human alliances.

Differences in the early Church were settled within the structure of callings in ministry. Never once did Church leaders take internal issues to the world to decide "right" and "wrong." We read about the issues of circumcision and Church discipline recorded in the Bible because such matters were discussed in letters addressed to Christians. Beyond the message of salvation, the entire New Testament was written only to believers.

The Apostle Paul wrote that the earth is groaning, waiting for the revealing or manifestation of the sons of God (Romans 8:19-25). This manifestation means a message of hope in answer to a groaning world. This manifestation is the true Church. Until the manifestation of sons and daughters of light, the earth staggers in its course, waiting for a voice of direction to say, "Jesus is the Way, the Truth and the Life!"

Is Jesus the Light of the world? Did He not also say that His Church is "a city set upon a hill"? The world waits in a valley of darkness for sure direction and some flicker of hope. The groaning of the earth mingles with the voices of martyrs crying under the altar of God, "How long, O Lord?" (Revelation 6:9,10). No agency on earth can answer this cry except the Church. Jesus said that the Church storms the gates of hell in victory. There is no way the Church can fail. If the Church fails, then God fails.

Yet, while cries ascend to God's throne for deliverance, many who speak as Christians cause spiritual abortion in the womb of the Church at a slaughter surpassing all other periods in Church history. Many

Christian leaders cry out against natural abortion, which is indeed one of the major sins of our generation. But an even greater sin is the killing of "little ones" sitting on church pews or watching Christian television programs featuring prophets crying out against the Church.

Babes in Christ are killed by traditions of men, form without power, and lack of sustaining nourishment from God's Word to help them grow and develop into spiritually mature soldiers. Warfare kills "little ones" who are ignorant of the wiles of Satan. God's people are destroyed for lack of knowledge. They are "tossed to and fro" as children, and many die along the way. They are killed by teachers who try to please the masses with a message of comforting sentiment instead of truth which presses young Christians toward mature, responsible Christianity.

Jesus' disciples wanted to call down fire from heaven on those who were preaching His message, but were not members of their immediate circle. Jesus rebuked His disciples. He said that those who were not against Him were for Him. Note that the only ones Jesus prophesied against were religious leaders standing at the door of the Kingdom and blocking others from entering. Never once did Jesus command those who were preaching "restoration" and "healing" to stop! Never once did He call anyone proclaiming "good news" a "heretic"! No, Jesus said, "Let them alone!" He knew that those bearing even portions of truth would be "fitly joined together" into one body to answer the groaning of the earth. He felt great compassion toward the cries of the world for truth. He knew that in unity, His light would shine through that city set upon a hill.

How sad is the indictment against a Church who

aborts her own babies in a day of groaning for deliverance. In a time of groaning before God for deliverance from bondage, Moses was born to the Hebrew nation. Male children were killed because Satan knew that God had heard the cry of His people for a deliverer. Likewise, Herod issued an edict to murder male Jewish children when he received word that a king was born and wise men had seen His star. Satan fears a time of crying out before God for a deliverer. Natural abortion and spiritual abortion are rampant in such a day. And such a day characterizes this generation!

Babes in Christ sit before television sets and are spiritually slaughtered by those standing at the door of the Kingdom. Instead of a message of hope, they hear upbraiding against men and women of God who preach the gospel of Christ. Not only are those who verbally attack godly servants under the judgment of Christ, but also the media who caters to messengers insuring them financial profits. Messages motivated by financial support spiritually abort God's people. Young Christians contribute money to causes which God never ordained. They are led to believe they are acting in obedience to God.

How do we settle our differences to protect "little ones"? Several months ago, Pastor Karl Strader of The Carpenter's Home Church in Lakeland, Florida, contacted me about some conflicts in our biblical perspectives. He asked if he could spend some time discussing those differences with me. After opening the Word of God together for several hours, we left knowing that we were brothers in Christ. No, we are not totally agreed on every point of doctrine, but we are "one" in knowing that Jesus Christ is Lord. The next month Karl Strader wrote in his newsletter that we are brothers. That is a powerful statement to the world—we are one Spirit in our Lord Jesus Christ! Our differences of opinion will not stand in the way of a "little one" searching for a message of hope, knocking at a door to find answers.

I must warn those spiritual leaders who refuse to address the controversy of our day that they will be pressed to take a stand. Recently, I heard a pastor hide behind a cloak of spirituality by saying, "All I preach is Jesus Christ, and Him crucified . . ." (1 Corinthians 2:2). However, on close examination of the text of that quote, the Apostle Paul made the statement in opposition to strict Judaism and the controversy of first century Christians attempting to compromise the gospel of Christ. That statement also confronted pagan societies to which Paul boldly announced that salvation in Christ is the only hope of man. Such a statement was never written to avoid confrontation, but to thrust one into the most intense warfare against any opposition to the gospel.

The "cross" and "Jesus Christ crucified" is the heart of God's strategy to redeem mankind. The cross is the theme of the Kingdom message. Only by redemption through Christ do we enter the Kingdom. The King is the focus of the Kingdom. The strategy of the cross is the center of the servants' message. Jesus is Lord over all circumstances of our lives. The cross means self-denial for the sake of seeking first His Kingdom. Embracing the cross gives Christians overcoming power. The Bible says that if Satan had understood the strategy of the cross, he would never have crucified the Lord. The cross is not an escape from warfare; it is the strategy of warfare. Instead of backing away by "preaching the cross," that theme becomes the two-edged sword of division between life and death of those who hear.

Another cloak of spirituality is when pastors say that every Christian needs to take his Bible and judge the truth for himself. This is not the instruction of God's Word. God gives the five-fold ministry for the "equipping of the saints" and the "edifying of the body" (Ephesians 4:12). Man has no right to private interpretation of the Word of God apart from those whom God sets in the Church as spiritual teachers and elders.

Are all Christians to become kings unto themselves? Many Christians are encouraged to be their own biblical authorities. But how will the body of Christ ever be "fitly joined together" with such independence of spirit? Jesus said, "You have ears, but do not hear . . ." Christians seek teachers to confirm their own opinions. This liberty is not given to individuals in the Church apart from anointed teachers called within the body. Men of old were moved upon by the Holy Spirit to record God's Word in manuscripts. Even so, God speaks today through those whom He has called to open the mysteries of His Word.

Many Bible commentators pose as pseudo-protectors of the Church. The obvious question is how can one "protect" and yet "expose" faults at the same time? On learning of her pregnancy, Joseph never exposed what he believed to be the faults of Mary, but in obedience to God, he covered her as a vessel chosen to produce the Deliverer. Likewise, the Church is God's voice in the world today as the only source of hope for a lost and dying world.

Pseudo-protectors must answer the question, "Under whose authority do you preach, teach and write?" I did not apologize for asking Jimmy Swaggart under whose authority he speaks messages of condemnation toward other brethren. Many fellow pastors are perplexed with his stand against Catholics and certain Christian ministers. I did not apologize to Dave Hunt in stating that I do not consider him to be a spiritual elder to the universal Church. Even as a researcher in the occult, I am persuaded that he needs spiritual covering for his own protection.

When Jesus met the centurion and commended his great faith, Jesus gave key insight into God's plan of spiritual covering and authority. Authority in the Kingdom of God is similar to the structure of command in the military. Some people are under us in authority, and some are over us. Those who issue commands must also receive commands. I question where pseudo-protectors of the Church receive their commands.

As a man under authority, I went to Baton Rouge, Louisiana. My only motive was to bring understanding of the Kingdom message to one with whom I am in covenant. My goal was to stand beside my brother in unity before the eyes of the world in the most fundamental, orthodox creeds which determine eternal life and death.

Jesus is the firstfruit among many brethren. As the firstfruit, He came to show us the way, the truth and the life. Because He is the "the Firstfruit," we are also branches of that vine, an integral part of the ongoing incarnation of God in the world. As He was in the world, so are we. Moses sent spies to report on the Promised Land that Israel had been given by God. Those spies brought fruit from the land—grapes, pomegranates, apples, etc. The "firstfruit" the spies brought promised that more could be found in the land. But the land had to be conquered! The enemy held the territory! Likewise, Jesus is the firstfruit of the Kingdom of God. We are that fruit now held behind enemy lines, but in the process of possessing the land. We represent fruit of hope, love, compassion, restoration and truth. But the land still must be conquered.

The call of the Church is to conquer the promised land from powers and principalities (Ephesians 6). The gates of hell shall not prevail against our conquest. The Church is not a failing institution! On the contrary, she is entering her most glorious hour! I strongly disagree with a statement in a letter written to me by Jimmy Swaggart the day after our meeting in Baton Rouge. He wrote, ". . . Instead of the church growing stronger and stronger as prognosticated, it will, instead, grow weaker and weaker (a falling away?) . . ." How can Evangelist Swaggart's statement be correct when God's Word teaches that "He that is within us is greater . . ."? Greater than what? Greater than powers and principalities, world systems, the kingdoms of this world!

The time has come for Christians to realize that the Church is not a failing institution! While the world grows worse and worse, the Church is maturing into a bride without spot and wrinkle. The Church is becoming the reflection of God's love for the world— the essence of John 3:16—so that those who believe in Jesus will not perish, but have everlasting life.

We must understand the reasons why the focus of attack from pseudo-protectors of the Church is aimed at prophets of hope. Obviously Satan would attack Oral Roberts. This man has brought the message of healing to the body of Christ. Oral Roberts allowed the anointing of healing gifts in his ministry to be used in bringing people to Jesus. Recently at our pastors' conference at Chapel Hill Harvester Church, the prophecy was given that Oral Roberts' healing ministry was now raised by God to a dimension to bring healing to the body of Christ. Even in that conference, Oral Roberts spoke boldly against racial and religious prejudices which separate Christians.

God has singularly lifted this man as a voice of unity to the body of Christ. Oral Roberts has been given the mission of sending medical teams to the most remote areas of the world. This responsibility called for Oral Roberts to be willing to sacrifice his own life to accomplish God's mandate to him. The Church, fitly joined together to finance this project, can give a message of hope and love to the world.

Obviously Satan would attack Jim Bakker. This man has built a city of refuge, has taken wayward and hopeless people off the streets, has offered homes to those who are physically handicapped, and has made all these people know they are an important part of God's plan. He has built a place of recreation for Christian families, a place of demonstration of God's goodness to man. Of course, Satan would use every means possible to discredit such a Kingdom demonstrator.

Obviously Satan would attack a gifted teacher like Charles Stanley. This pastor has become a leading spokesman for Southern Baptists. Because God has used this man as an example of a pastor in a growing, thriving church in Atlanta's inner city, he stood between warring factions in his denomination as a peacemaker.

Obviously Satan would attack Robert Schuller. Dr. Schuller's message of hope reaches to people in the worst conditions of life and lifts their hearts in realizing their value as God's creation. He points to Jesus as the restorer of man to God's image. His message stirs within us the possibilities of our potential in the Lord. Of course Satan battles such a message.

Obviously Satan would attack Kenneth Copeland. This man has brought the body of Christ to an understanding of covenant with God and the kind of faith Abraham knew in implementing that covenant. No wonder he and his wife, Gloria, are attacked as "seducers." Satan battles any message crying out to the world that faith will overcome defeat and despair.

Obviously Satan would attack John and Paula Sanford. They bring an understanding of inner healing to the body of Christ, ministering in a society filled with emotional pain. The world cries with emotional and spiritual abuse and bruises. Of course Satan battles anyone with answers to desperate needs in people's lives.

Obviously Satan would attack Paul and Jan Crouch who are using the media as a means of taking the gospel of the Kingdom to the world. Their message offers the hope of abundant life as a direct result of prosperity in the soul. This couple is reaching out to people in the United States as well as countries desperately needing the light of the gospel because of oppressive conditions of government and political unrest.

Obviously Satan would attack Paul Yonggi Cho, a man leading thousands of people to Christ and calling them to commitment in intercession. His innovative "cell groups" concept has made personalized ministry possible in churches with thousands of members.

Obviously Satan would attack Pastor Larry Lea whom God has given the message of prayer and church growth. When men are called to pull down

Satan's strongholds in the heavenlies and begin teaching others the power of loosing and binding in intercession, of course they will be attacked, maligned, discredited and slandered.

An attack rages against prophets of hope by pseudo-protectors of the Church who become the spokesmen for thousands of people. Such attacks produce fruit of fear, doubt and suspicion among brothers and sisters in Christ. But at the same time, many Christians are growing in unity of faith into the full stature of Christ—a fully matured bride prepared to do warfare against satanic forces.

Jesus lived as the human representative of the Godhead. Christ is the complete expression of the Father (Hebrews 1). Even so, Christ breathed upon His Church to give us His authority and power which is above all others. This transfer of authority was completed on the Day of Pentecost when the Holy Spirit descended upon the Church. The resident power of the Holy Spirit assures that we are the Church who cannot fail. The New Testament does not raise the issue whether the Church will fail; the Church cannot fail!

God has given us the Holy Spirit as our seal of promise, and we become responsible for showing the world the way, the truth and the life. Anyone exposing the weaknesses or frailties of the human vessels whom God has trusted with the gift of His Spirit is no friend to the cause of God. The purpose of this book is to examine the differences between the real and the counterfeit. Differences do exist in the body of Christ, but God is calling for peacemakers in this day of dissension and violence. We must focus on an agreement that Jesus Christ is Lord!

While some people accuse Kingdom teachers of

being humanistic and minimizing the prominence of Jesus, the opposite of that accusation is actually true. I am shocked that Jimmy Swaggart listened to an explanation of my theological perspective and then drew this conclusion! Those who recognize Jesus as King and Lord of the coming Kingdom place Him where He rightfully belongs according to the final chapters of Revelation. Such a realization of Christ rejuvenates the Church at a time when mammon and world systems are failing to solve their dilemmas.

The majority of "doom" prophets view the Roman Catholic Church as the harlot church of Revelation. Most of them refuse to associate with Spirit-filled Catholics, even those with the evidence of the Holy Spirit in their lives and ministries. I contend that religious systems are the harlot church. The harlot church is never composed of born-again, Spirit-filled Christians.

Who dares accuse Father Bertolucci of heresy because he honors the Virgin Mary with a reverence which is uncomfortable to many other Christians? Who has been given the right to judge his views of spiritual authority? In a recent visit to the campus of Steubenville University, I found that the majority of those Catholic students were filled with the power of the Holy Spirit. I spoke with Father Scanlon and found a deeply spiritual Christian leader who longs for unity in the body of Christ. Last summer as one of nine Charismatic pastors participating in the Roman Catholic/Pentecostal Dialogue, I found Catholic leaders to be men and women seeking the truth of God's Word with all their hearts.

The Church must stand boldly today in claiming the promises of John 17, "Father, make them one . . ." Jesus left the Church with a prayer that we become one Spirit in Him. We are commissioned, pressed and challenged to come into unity of Spirit for one reason . . . **that the world may know!**

2

PEACEMAKERS

Jesus said that "peacemakers" are blessed people. In fact, though the term itself is controversial these days, Jesus said that peacemakers would be called "sons of God." Why? One of three ingredients of the Kingdom of God is peace, along with righteousness and joy (Romans 14:17). In fact, peace is listed between righteousness and joy because it is the pivotal quality of the Kingdom. Righteousness, which is right living according to instructions in God's Word, produces peace. Inner peace brings continuous, unconditional joy into believers' lives. Any person whose life exemplifies the Kingdom of God will be one who pursues peace and brings peaceful solutions to turbulent circumstances.

God loves peace. He loves peace so much that one of the seven things God hates listed in Proverbs is "discord among brethren" (Proverbs 6:19). Jesus is called "The Prince of Peace," though His life and ministry constantly upset people who were opposed to His teaching. The love which Jesus commanded His disciples to demonstrate as a witness requires Christians to make peace with one another. Love and peacemaking go together, and Jesus does not make them optional qualities for His Church.

Yet Christians are geared to expect divisions and strife. We have been conditioned by a sick society that thrives on controversy. From political mud-slinging on the news, to Norman Lear comedy shows, our living rooms are bombarded with contention every evening through television. We accept discord as a way of life. Christians become far more comfortable debating one another than facing the world in agreement. We express our differences easier than our similarities. We are seasoned skeptics through educational philosophies and the influence of the media. We find trusting one another difficult or even impossible. Peacemakers called to a ministry of reconciliation are regarded as either "do-gooders" lacking conviction because we don't understand the issues, or progressive liberals crying "peace at any price."

I've contemplated the irony of war. Wars are fought to bring peace. Wars in our hearts are often generated by something as simple as a barking dog in the neighborhood keeping us awake at night. War and peace are both qualities of the heart which spill into our circumstances, relationships and choices throughout life. Every Christian must learn the discipline of removing irritations that come our way so that our spirits remain clear to express Christ within us. If the Kingdom of God is "peace in the Holy Spirit," we cannot allow grievances to build in our hearts. Otherwise, we forfeit our ability to express God's Kingdom in our lives.

Both love and peace are fruit of the Holy Spirit. The seeds of that fruit are easily planted in the lives of others. Because our world is characterized by such contention, people who express peace truly shine with God's glory. They attract others because the quality of peace offers security to people who are troubled.

Though it seems like a contradiction, peacemakers are strong warriors against evil. The gospel of peace confronts bondage from Satan. A Christian who brings a spirit of peace into stormy circumstances is the one who is in charge. Jesus spoke to the wind and waves in a storm at sea by saying, "Peace! Be still!" We must understand that love and peace are forces with God's authority which overcome contrary winds.

Peace is part of our full armor in warfare. Our feet are shod with the preparation of the gospel of peace (Ephesians 6:15). That verse means that we go into battle prepared to bring peace—because God's authority within us will win the battle! Paul writes, "Let the peace of Christ rule in your hearts to which indeed you were called in one body . . ." Paul writes to Timothy, ". . . pursue righteousness, faith, love, peace with those who call on the Lord out of a pure heart" (2 Timothy 2:22). The writer of Hebrews issues a stern admonition, "Pursue peace with all men, and holiness, without which no one will see the Lord" (Hebrews 12:14).

I believe in pursuing peace. I had requested to meet

with Evangelist Jimmy Swaggart in response to an article, "The Coming Kingdom," which he wrote and published in his monthly magazine, *The Evangelist*. Evangelist Swaggart quoted me several times in the article and warned of the dangers of "Kingdom Age" teaching (a term Jimmy Swaggart uses which includes New Kingdom, Restoration, Restitution, Manifest Sons, Rebuilding the Tabernacle of David, Third Wave Theology, New Wave Revival, Kingdom Now, Latter Rain, etc.). I have given some details of that meeting with both Jimmy Swaggart and author Dave Hunt, but now I will address the issues which brought about the meeting.

I began by telling the Swaggart staff that I had not prepared notes nor a theological presentation, but I sensed that God was in charge of the meeting. I believed strongly that something very special would result from our willingness to come to a mutual understanding of one another's views. I was grateful to Jimmy Swaggart for allowing me the opportunity to come to Baton Rouge and to address such a notable assembly. I stated that I was especially grateful for Evangelist Swaggart's arranging for me to meet Dave Hunt. I added that since both of the men had written about me, the time had come for them to talk to me!

Then I gave three reasons for requesting the meeting with Jimmy Swaggart. First, I said that I recognized from the article in *The Evangelist*, and subsequent television broadcasts on his daily, "A Study in God's Word" program, in which my books were quoted and my ministry was discussed, that my teaching on the Kingdom had become an "offense" to Jimmy Swaggart. I knew that some of the conclusions which Evangelist Swaggart had drawn con-

cerning Kingdom teaching were simply misunderstandings which demanded clarification directly
from me.

On the basis of clarification, I stated that I
intended to follow the directions of Matthew 5:23,24,
"Therefore if you bring your gift to the altar, and
there remember that your brother has something
against you, leave your gift there before the altar,
and go your way. First be reconciled to your brother,
and then come and present your gift." Let me point
out that Christians often misread the instructions in
that verse. It does not say if you have an offense
against someone; it says that if your brother has
something against you . . . go . . . be reconciled.

Secondly, I felt a responsibility to give a clear
answer regarding areas of biblical interpretation in
which I disagree with Evangelist Swaggart. I quoted
1 Peter 3:15, "But sanctify the Lord God in your
hearts, and always be ready to give a defense to
everyone who asks you a reason for the hope that is
in you, with meekness and fear . . ." We agreed in
some areas in which he believed we were opposed,
and some of our theological differences were not the
heresy he believed them to be.

Since Jimmy Swaggart is unquestionably an elder
in the body of Christ, I emphasized that I must
account for our differences with an attempt at bringing understanding and unity. I told Evangelist
Swaggart that I regarded him and Oral Roberts as
two of the most influential men in the Church today.
I reminded Jimmy Swaggart that the opportunity for
such great influence presented him with a major
responsibility in moving people toward peaceful resolutions of disputes.

Finally, I reminded the gathering that we share a

common enemy in secular humanism. I pointed out that an attack on the standards of the Church by men such as television producer Norman Lear, and civil action suits against religious expression promoted by groups such as the A.C.L.U. made disagreements within the ranks of the Church even more threatening and diversionary.

I called for us to join together in a unified front according to John 17:21, "... that they all may be one ... that the world may believe that You sent Me." Often I have pleaded for Church leaders to meet behind closed doors for dialogue on their differences so that Christians could face the enemies of the gospel as a united group.

Then I answered the charges published in *The Evangelist* article against my teaching. Many were the same points which Dave Hunt raises in *Seduction of Christianity*. I will devote entire chapters in this book to some of these points which I feel directly impact the Kingdom message that God has given me to proclaim to the body of Christ. Now I will simply give a synopsis of my answers to these charges as I spoke them at the meeting in Baton Rouge.

First I addressed the issue of biblical authority. The article stated, "The teaching of the Kingdom Agers tends to produce low regard for the authority of the Bible. According to their teachings, man's thoughts and personal revelations take precedence over the Word. (And this is probably the most dangerous part of this teaching.)" (Swaggart, Jimmy, "The Coming Kingdom," *The Evangelist*, vol. 18; no. 9, [September 1986], p.8).

In answer to this charge, I strongly denied the accusation from my own theological perspective. I insisted that my theology was orthodox Christianity according to historical creeds of the Church: The Apostles' Creed, the Nicene Creed, for example. I strongly affirmed my belief that the sixty-six books of the Bible are a closed canon—God's recorded truth to man which carries final authority, and which is interpreted only by the guidance of the Holy Spirit. In regard to theological interpretations, I stated that man's revelation must always be judged according to the authority of God's recorded Word.

Next I addressed the topic of "unity," about which Jimmy Swaggart's article states, "The biggest 'message' today of the Kingdom Agers is the message of 'unity.' Basically anything is accepted. The occultists and modernists are accepted as long as there is no criticism of the 'unity' or 'Kingdom Age' message." (Swaggart, p.8). I emphasized that this accusation concerning "unity" is not only untrue, but also vicious and unjust! I believe that such statements demonstrate irresponsible leadership and are damaging to the cause of God in the world today.

The next area I addressed was the charge that I disregarded elders judging prophecy because I said that no one "judges prophets." Jimmy Swaggart's article (p.7) had quoted from my book, *The Wounded Body of Christ*, (K-Dimension Publishers, 1st edition, 1983, p.31), "There is no judging by elders of the voice of the prophet if he or she is God's called-out man or woman speaking as a prophet. If he is called as a prophet, there is no need for judging or proof because the ministry must prove itself."

I answered this misunderstanding over "judging prophecy" by stating that of course prophetic utterances are judged by elders to determine their agreement with the Word of God and a common witness of the Holy Spirit among eldership. The Spirit of prophecy demonstrated as a gift to the Church must always be judged. However, though prophecy is judged, the prophet is not. The Apostle Paul stated that he did not "confer with flesh and blood." Jesus told Peter that "flesh and blood has not revealed this to you, but My Father Who is in heaven."

I further explained that "judging prophecy" as referred to in 1 Corinthians 14:29 focused on judging the "weighty matters" of the prophecy. No man has been called to judge whether John the Baptist, Elijah or Jimmy Swaggart are spokesmen for God to His people. I asked Jimmy Swaggart whether he called Springfield (Assembly of God headquarters) before he spoke a prophetic utterance in his ministry as a world-wide evangelist.

Another charge I answered concerned the concept of "Kingdom now" as opposed to the dispensational teaching of a literal "thousand year reign" of Christ. The article states (p.8), "The Kingdom Agers teach that the church establishes the Kingdom before Christ returns. Earl Paulk says that the church will establish the Kingdom and then, when it is finally established, will welcome the Lord back to take over an already-established Kingdom."

I pointed out the difference in the world that "God loves" (John 3:16) and the world systems that will "pass away" (1 John 2:15-17). I explained my view that as Babylon (world systems) falls, the Church will mature into a spiritually discerning bride. I believe the Church provides the standard of witness by which God will judge the world and the ruler of this world (John 16:11). I denied that I have ever taught that the world is getting better and better and everyone will be a Christian when Jesus returns.

Another area of explanation focused on "little

gods." Both Jimmy Swaggart's article (p.11) and Dave Hunt's *Seduction of Christianity* quoted from my book, *Satan Unmasked* (K-Dimension Publishers, 1st edition, pp.96,97), "Just as dogs have puppies and cats have kittens, God has little gods. Until we comprehend that we are gods, and begin to act like little gods, we can't manifest the Kingdom of God."

I explained that my teaching differentiates between being "like God" and being created in "the image of God." In the Garden of Eden, Satan tempted Eve to become "like God." As "little gods," people establish a self-centered base of authority just as Lucifer did when he attempted to ascend to God's throne.

I pointed out that Jesus is the perfect example of humanity living in the "image of God" in perfect obedience and harmony with the Father. Through Christ, man is given the opportunity to regain his identity as being created in "the image of God," though he still sins and needs forgiveness and daily "washing by the Word" until Jesus returns. I believe that the identity of man "created in the image of God" is Paul's meaning in Ephesians 4:13, ". . . till we all come to the unity of the faith and the knowledge of the Son of God, to a perfect man, to the measure of the stature of the fullness of Christ." I also challenged Dave Hunt that the only alternative to believing that man was created "in God's image" is to accept the theory of evolution, which I assumed Mr. Hunt did not believe.

The final area which I answered concerned the charge that my ministry was anti-Semitic. Swaggart wrote (pp.8,9), "Some have an anti-semitism slant, which is a doctrine of contempt for the Jews." I answered by not only denying the charge, but also pointing out the prominent place of the natural Jew in prophecy throughout the Bible. I affirmed my belief that God is and will graft in the natural olive branch into the Vine, Jesus Christ. I added that the responsibility for spiritual revival among Jews rests with the prayers and witness of the Church. Then I reminded the gathering that the Apostle Paul did not instruct the Church to pray for the "peace of Jerusalem," but for the "salvation of Israel" (Romans 10:1). I also added that many blessings are not received today because people are not instructed on blessing spiritual Israel, the "good ground ministries" of the Church.

After a brief recess, Dave Hunt responded to my remarks, focusing primarily on the teaching of "little gods" and a "man-centered theology," which I believe to be unorthodox and cultish as much as Dave Hunt does. Then the assembly asked me questions concerning my beliefs and my ministry at Chapel Hill Harvester Church in Atlanta.

The conclusion of the meeting was very positive. I offered to extend our discussion to further dialogue, and/or state my beliefs on Evangelist Swaggart's daily television Bible study. I also extended an open invitation to Jimmy Swaggart to preach at Chapel Hill Harvester Church in Atlanta which I would be delighted to honor.

The next week I received a cordial letter from Jimmy Swaggart in which he wrote, "First of all I want to once again express my appreciation to you for the time taken to come to Baton Rouge to discuss matters of importance pertaining to the Kingdom of God . . . (In reference to Tommy Reid's coming) I only wish we would have had time for more fellowship . . . I want to commend you on your actions, the definitions of your faith, and your statements made in the excellent spirit they were given. We could not have asked for more or better. Possibly in the future there will be time for more dialogue. I feel these are always good . . ." The letter continued by pointing out again the areas in which he feels we have fundamental theological differences. I respond to those comments with sadness, but also with confidence in knowing that both Jimmy Swaggart and I love and talk to the same Father. I trust the Lord with matters beyond my own understanding (Proverbs 3:5,6). I believe His Word that tells me, "Having done all, stand . . ." (Ephesians 6:13).

I believe Satan wars unity of Christian leaders with all the forces at his command because of the strength derived from spiritual unity in Christ. But true peacemakers do not depend upon the response of others to pursue peace. God did not make pursuing peace optional. Peace is a major goal of our warfare. "And another horse, fiery red, went out. And it was granted to the one who sat on it to take peace from the earth, and that people should kill one another; and there was given to him a great sword" (Revelation 6:4). The good news is that God gives an unfailing sword to His peacemakers. Jesus said, "Peace I leave with you, My peace I give to you; not as the world gives do I give to you" (John 14:27). Jesus is the source of our peace. Because He is our source, peacemakers must leave the results of their obedience in pursuing peace to the working of the Holy Spirit.

Who judges the hearts of men? What man can claim the right of judging ministries? Scriptures regarding man's right to judge others hardly give Christians freedom in expressing subjective opinions. God's Word alone remains our absolute source of righteous discernment. Yet, the Scriptures themselves seem to give conflicting instructions on a believer's right to judge others.

Jesus clearly warned against judging "the speck" in others' eyes while failing to see "the plank" in one's own (Matthew 7:1-5). God admonishes us by saying, "Vengeance is Mine, I will repay . . ." (Deuteronomy 32:35; Hebrews 10:30; Romans 12:19). Jesus warned that the standards by which we judge others set the requirements of judgment we impose upon ourselves (Matthew 7:2). Even forgiveness from God for transgressions against us depends upon our willingness to forgive others (Matthew 6:12).

On the other hand Jesus instructed His followers, "Do not judge according to appearance, but judge with righteous judgment" (John 7:24). The Apostle Paul also exhorted the Church to learn how to execute righteous judgment in settling their disputes. He encouraged Christians to prepare for judging the world and angels (1 Corinthians 6:1-7). Paul demonstrated judgment in his own ministry. He instructed the Church at Corinth to disfellowship members who practiced immoral conduct (1 Corinthians 5:9-13). Paul corrected Peter and other apostles and elders over the issue of circumcision (Acts 15). Paul disagreed with Barnabas over taking Mark with them to Syria, causing a rift between the two apostles for a period of time.

Disputes among Christians are hardly confined to the contemporary Church. However, the history of controversy in the Church does not ease the pain of theological discord nor diminish the struggle of exercising righteous judgment for the sake of peace. All believers go to the Scriptures seeking truth of the Holy Spirit. We all agree that God's judgments are absolute and undefiled. But even when quoting Scripture passages to justify our views, too often men's interpretations become clouded by their own theological perspectives. So how do we discern truth in controversy?

Like many other ministers of the gospel of Jesus Christ, I've wrestled in my own spirit with the explosive issues of controversy entangling evangelical Christians in debate. Spiritual discernment and guidance from the Lord is paramount for those of us who are charged with leading others in spiritual growth. Accountability to God for the lives of others demands that Christian leaders walk circumspectly in their understanding.

Though the numerous issues of contention are hardly confined to one writer or book, Dave Hunt and T. A. McMahon's *The Seduction of Christianity* certainly merits careful consideration of the issues it raises for two reasons: First, Hunt and McMahon's book is widely read by evangelical Christians. Wide distribution of their book carries great potential for influence toward ministries the writers either approve or repudiate.

Secondly, Hunt and McMahon's book raises viable issues for dialogue in the twentieth century Church. Most of the concerns the writers express do deserve consideration and scriptural answers. Some of the writers' concerns are valid dangers that are infiltrating orthodox Christian doctrine. Based on those concerns, the writers are certainly entitled to publish their warnings.

However, problems with this particular theological treatise become apparent from the opening paragraphs. Hunt examines contemporary Christian teaching he considers to be error by quoting numerous ministers who he believes threaten the Church.

31

He selects quotes from these ministers to substantiate his warnings. Hunt even accuses certain men and women in ministry of combining Christianity and "sorcery." According to Mr. Hunt, these teachers' perspectives either are or are becoming unorthodox and occult in their goals.

I admit that I do not totally agree in practice nor in doctrine with some of the reputable teachers under Mr. Hunt's fire in *Seduction of Christianity*. I even agree with Dave Hunt's assessment of dangers in certain cults he names. After all, Dave Hunt is identified by his publisher as being an expert on cults. His knowledge of occult practices is reported to be extensive. He researched the occult while living in India. He rightly identifies dangers and errors in the teaching of such humanistic philosophies as those espoused by men such as Napoleon Hill and groups such as the New Age. He is also correct in pointing out the infiltration of Eastern mysticism into religion and our society through the teaching of Yoga, Mormonism, the Church of Religious Science, and others.

Still, I am troubled by the prospect of any writer quoting numerous Christian ministers along with a host of mystics and cult leaders, all branded under the banner of "seduction." Such accusations demand examination. Mr. Hunt's own theological perspective becomes significant if we are to consider such serious charges as those he makes against others' ministries. Mr. Hunt's calling from God as judge of ministries becomes a viable issue if indeed God has given him that responsibility. Readers must decide whether the writer is in error in some of his views, or the ministers he accuses of teaching error are truly a threat to Christendom—and especially to "little ones" of the Kingdom. Undoubtedly, Christians directly embroiled in this controversy need to dedicate themselves to the restoration of others for the sake of our witness to the world.

Christ gave the Church the commission to proclaim the gospel of the Kingdom to every creature and to disciple all nations. The true enemy of God's will on earth is not flesh and blood. Spiritual forces of darkness work diligently to wrestle away the callings from those who have received God's direction for their lives, especially if they also lead others.

Spiritual warfare is real, intense, but also very subtle. One strategy Satan uses is to create a smoke screen, a mirage of danger within the ranks of the Church. Often a mirage gains credence and momentum from well-meaning Christians who are genuinely sincere in their concerns. Internal strife calls attention from real enemies in order to fight illusive foes. Rather than Christians' unifying our strength against the powers and principalities of darkness who oppose God's will, we turn our attention to examining other born-again believers with suspicion. The army of God divides. In confusion, the authority to fulfill God's will through His Church is snatched away.

God's Word is the basis of all true spiritual authority. The Bible, the Scripture, the Old Covenant Law and the New Covenant of salvation and grace is our primary source of guidance and discernment. God's Word to man never contradicts itself. The Scriptures are a trajectory out of which man's direction in his present circumstances must be totally consistent with the Spirit of God, the recorded Word of God, and the character of Jesus Christ, Who is the living Word. But remember that holy men of God wrote the Scriptures under the inspiration and guidance of the Holy Spirit. God consistently uses human vessels as spokesmen to His people.

No answer to charges of "seduction" is more critical than clearly defining the role of the Church in the world. The Church's mission establishes the basis for a person's calling in ministry. Claims of one's calling from God are meaningless unless the source and power of that calling is found in the commission of Jesus Christ to His Church. Our goal is to accomplish His purposes in us and through us as His witnesses. The diverse work of ministry shares one source of authority and power. Jesus described Himself as the Vine. Christians are numerous, distinct branches of that Vine (John 15:1-6). Another way to define the Church is the "body" of Christ. We function as diverse parts of one body (1 Corinthians 12:12-27).

Jesus gave callings to the Church in five categories (apostle, prophet, evangelist, pastor and teacher) to equip Christians for the work of the ministry. The five-fold ministry is responsible for guiding God's covenant people into unity of faith and spiritual maturity, "the fullness of the stature of Christ." This imagery—the fullness of the stature of Christ—is of great significance in understanding the purpose of the Church in the world. The primary mission of men and women called by God to serve in the five-fold ministry is to bring about the reality of Jesus' prayer, "That they may be one, as You, Father, are in Me, and I in You; that they also may be one in Us, that the world may believe that You sent Me" (John 17:21).

Jesus' prayer is not the call to organizational oneness. Rather, we are called to oneness in Christ. Christian oneness is built on the foundation of truth from God's Word. Unity, in spite of our diversity of doctrines and forms, is not only possible among Christians, it is essential to manifesting our witness of Jesus Christ to the world. Dogmatic factions among Christians have been the greatest detriment to our witness. We fight each other instead of our real enemies: the forces of Satan, humanistic ideologies, social abuse, etc. Internal fights destroy our credibility and voice. Yet Jesus said, "By this all men will know that you are My disciples, if you have love for one another" (John 13:35).

But how can Christians know whether one speaks truth today? What men can Christians really trust to give answers genuinely from God? The mark of spiritual maturity is discernment. We are told to ". . . test the spirits, whether they are of God; because many false prophets have gone out into the world" (1 John 4:1). An accusing spirit is never of God. Satan is the accuser, still accusing believers just as he stood before God accusing Job (Job 1:9-11).

Anyone correcting ministers of the gospel must carefully examine his motives. He must be sure that he speaks in the Spirit of Christ—bringing peace, healing and correction rather than accusations. Even answers to critics who warn against my own teaching must come only when God commands me to speak. I want to be careful not to fall guilty of becoming an offense to those whom I answer. Accountability in such weighty spiritual matters is both to God and to man. There is a time to be silent, and a time to speak (Ecclesiastes 3:7). God has commanded me to answer now, and I walk circumspectly before Him in this responsibility. The desire of my heart is to be a peacemaker while at the same time remaining firm and uncompromising in defending sound doctrine. One whom God calls to speak must stand solidly for truth against all opposition. Truth is judged according-ing to God's recorded Word, the unction of the Holy Spirit, and the fruit of one's labor. The ultimate goal of correction is to accomplish God's will by bringing reconciliation and unity.

Discerning Christians must ask themselves: Do the teachers whom Dave Hunt quotes as teaching error reveal the character of God? Are they branches of the Vine, Jesus Christ? Do they live as well as speak in His Spirit according to His Word? Do they bear spiritual fruit that brings glory to God? Do they create trust and faith toward God in the lives of Christians following their teaching? Does their teaching promote abundant life which pleases God? Are they peacemakers? John wrote:

> By this you know the Spirit of God: Every spirit that confesses that Jesus Christ has come in the flesh is of God, and every spirit that does not confess that Jesus Christ has come in the flesh is not of God. And this is the spirit of the Antichrist, which you have heard was coming, and is now already in the world. (1 John 4:2,3)

Jesus Christ has come in the flesh. He ministers today through His Church in the world, a Church embroiled in turmoil, mixture and strife. But the Church is maturing and being purified in warfare. Jesus will return for a mature, holy bride. She will greet Him as the five wise virgins who waited expectantly for Him. Their lamps were trimmed and burning with oil (Matthew 25:1-13).

Until Christ returns, God allows all that can be shaken to be shaken (Hebrew 12:26-29). This inevitable shaking includes all doctrines and liturgical rhetoric not based on truth from the Lord. Satan's time is short. God has unleashed His righteous judgment to make way for His eternal Kingdom to be manifested through His Church on earth. Righteous judgment begins at the house of God! In such perilous days, we must be certain that our lamps are trimmed and burning with oil.

Amid controversy, no benefit of God's presence within one's heart is more comforting than His covenant of peace. I refuse to back away from Jesus' prayer, ". . . that they all may be one, as You, Father, are in Me, and I in You; that the world may believe that You sent Me" (John 17:21). Peace begins in an individual's heart, and then Kingdom righteousness, peace and joy begins to infiltrate and influence our homes, our society and our world.

God sent His peace into the world. On a dark night near the town of Bethlehem, shepherds guarded their sheep. The world was in turmoil then as now. People were groping for meaning, lost and without hope. Perhaps the shepherds discussed the circulating rumors of the town or they argued their own views on the religious debates of their day. Suddenly, angels filled the night sky with bright light. One angel announced the birth of a King. Then all the heavenly host joined together to make a pronouncement that would impact the lives of those shepherds and the course of history. They exclaimed, "Glory to God in the highest! And on earth peace, good will toward men!"

And by God's grace, I receive His gift of peace to the world. I join the heavenly host in proclaiming the peace of God on earth within me. I share the joy among my brethren who heed the words of those angels by making room in their hearts for the Prince of Peace.

37

3

THE REAL AND THE COUNTERFEIT

Sincerity is not a criterion for truth. We live in a world filled with sincere people who are deceived. Certain religions demand stringent disciplines from worshipers, yet the people themselves live in spiritual darkness. Mothers in pagan societies have fed their children to crocodiles to appease an angry god. People have worn fish hooks in their bodies to purify themselves in religious rituals. Communist and Marxist radicals put the dedication of many born-again Christians to shame by their sacrifices to promote an atheistic religion.

Deceived people are always religious and sincere. In many cases, scribes and Pharisees challenged

Jesus with sincere adherence to the Mosaic Law. Initially perhaps, they believed the young teacher needed correction on such things as observing the Sabbath, ceremonial washing and discriminating relationships. But as they encountered the Spirit of Truth Himself, their legalism became obvious to all who heard the discussions.

Instead of ignoring their pompous correction, Jesus, "the Real," confronted religious hypocrites, "the counterfeit," with a choice. He fulfilled the Spirit of the Law, setting people free from oppression and giving them abundant life. Scripture reveals that few of the religious leaders ever repented and chose release from their bondage to pride. Instead, they hated the Healer from Nazareth more and more. While obsessively defending their interpretations of the "Law," they sought for an opportunity to kill the Way, the Truth and the Life.

One of Satan's most effective tools to make people reject "the real" is to cause them to fear a "counterfeit." Scripture teaches that "God has not given us a spirit of fear" (2 Timothy 1:7). Fear closes channels of spiritual power by countering our faith. The mixture of faith and fear never accomplishes anything for God. Faith and fear cannot co-exist within an individual for long; one or the other quickly wins. Choosing to follow either fear or faith determines our direction of action. We are forced to choose. Satan's oldest and most effective strategy for keeping people in deception is to make them afraid of the source of their help.

God instructed Moses to return to Egypt and lead Israel out of bondage (Exodus 4). We know the story of how Moses offered excuses to God. This great "deliverer" hardly saw himself as anything more than a shepherd. To boost Moses' confidence that he could do what God had asked him, God told Moses to throw his rod on the ground. Immediately, the rod became a serpent. What did Moses do? He ran in fear. He backed away, fearing his source of help—the only source of power that could bring the nation of Israel out of bondage.

Moses obeyed God and returned to Egypt on his mission. The episodes of Moses' confrontations with Pharaoh and the succession of miracles and plagues, some which were duplicated by the sorcery of Pharaoh's magicians, is truly a study in the contrasts of "the real" and "the counterfeit." Nevertheless, Moses grew in confidence as God performed His Word. The same man who ran in fear from God's display of power now stood in obedience to the Lord. In confidence, Moses boldly challenged Pharaoh to his face.

We might think that people would be delighted at witnessing miracles, signs and wonders of God. Most people run in fear. While some catch the spirit of God's liberating power and become vessels of service in Christ's Kingdom, others back away. For example, Jesus cast out violent demons from a man roaming the tombs near Galilee. The demons entreated Jesus by saying, "If You are going to cast us out, send us into the herd of swine." Jesus cast them out, and immediately the herd of swine rushed into the sea, perishing in the water (Luke 8:26-33).

The verses following the account of this deliverance are very interesting.

When those who fed them [the swine] saw what had happened, they fled and told it in the city and in the country. Then they went out to see what had happened, and came to Jesus, and found the man from whom the demons had departed, sitting at the feet of Jesus,

41

*clothed and in his right mind. **And they were afraid.**
They also who had seen it told them by what means he
who had been demon-possessed was healed. Then the
whole multitude of the surrounding region of the Gada-
renes asked Him to depart from them, for **they were
seized with great fear.** And He got into the boat and
returned. Now the man from whom the demons had
departed begged Him that He might be with Him. But
Jesus sent him away, saying, "Return to your own
house, and tell what great things God has done for
you." And he went his way and proclaimed throughout
the whole city what great things Jesus had done for
him. (Luke 8:34-39)*

Fear of God's true anointed power continued in the
ministry of the apostles. Two members of the church,
Ananias and his wife, Sapphira, lied to the Holy
Spirit about the sale of some property they owned.
Both fell dead at the apostles' feet.

*So **great fear came upon all the church and upon
all who heard these things.** And through the hands
of the apostles many signs and wonders were done
among the people. And they were all with one accord in
Solomon's porch. Yet none of the rest dared join them,
but the people esteemed them highly. And believers were
increasingly added to the Lord, multitudes of both men
and women . . . (Acts 5:11-14)*

The Spirit of God moves in power. Multitudes of
people are saved, healed, set free from bondages and
filled with joy in the Holy Spirit. Immediately, fearmongers rush in with severe warnings. A few voices
speaking in fear can control a mob. Satan has no
new tactics. Just as numerous examples are recorded
in Scripture, much of the controversy in the Church
today is motivated by fear of "the real."

Satan even attempts to use "the counterfeit" to a
dual advantage. Some people are deceived and lost.

Others recognize that Satan creates a "counterfeit." In their caution at recognizing the possibility of error in the Church, they reject any teaching that they cannot understand. These Christians follow the old adage of "throwing out the baby with the bath water." They suspect that everything and everyone moving in ways they do not understand may be false. Consequently, their spiritual growth is thwarted by fear of the unknown. They hold on to safety in easily understood biblical precepts, but they never grow in faith. They never "walk on the water" in spiritual demonstration of God's Word.

Dave Hunt's *Seduction of Christianity* could easily plant such fear in the hearts of Christians today. The focus of many of his warnings pinpoint ministries teaching "faith" as a weapon for confronting circumstances in daily living. He cites Robert Tilton, Charles Capps, Fred Price and a host of others as promoting dangerously positive expectations in Christians' hearts and minds (Hunt, p.84). Of course extremes always occur in implementation of biblical principles. I question Mr. Hunt's caution, however, since God must either confirm, deny or ignore our petitions of faith. God must answer. We don't.

We must recognize that Satan's greatest attack is aimed against those moving mightily under the anointed power of God. Satan, the father of lies, will use any strategy to kill a witness to God's glory. He trembles at God's plan of reaping a great harvest in these last days. Babylon, world systems, will fall. Simultaneously, God's people will shine like the sun (Isaiah 60:1-3). Covenant people offer solutions through the power of Christ within them. Let's examine specific areas of "the real" and "the counterfeit" clashing in the Church today.

The wisdom of God is real; the mind of reason, humanism, is the counterfeit. I discuss "biblical humanism" extensively in subsequent chapters. Let me emphasize simply that Satan construes the Word of God to his advantage. Satan quoted Scripture to Jesus on the Mount of Temptation (Matthew 4:5,6). He used the Scripture to reason with Jesus and appeal to His desires (lust of the flesh, lust of the eyes, the pride of life). Satan uses spiritual pride and the mind of reason far more effectively to trap mature Christians than promises of prosperity and wealth. Jesus was attacked by scribes and Pharisees who came to Him with accusations based on the letter of the Law (John 8:3-11). Satan used the controversy over circumcision to separate Christians in the early Church. Humanism, the mind of reason, always offers seemingly sensible direction and reasonable explanations. It also destroys sensitivity to the Holy Spirit.

Wisdom of God is discerned only by the Holy Spirit. God's wisdom is foolishness to the natural mind. God said in Isaiah, " 'For My thoughts are not your thoughts, nor are your ways My ways,' says the Lord" (Isaiah 55:8). The strategy of the cross is absurd to natural reasoning. Many times if we "reason out" directions from God, we lose the faith to act by the power of the Holy Spirit. Paul said, "For as many as are led by the Spirit of God, these are sons of God" (Romans 8:14). We can read God's Word, hear sermons, pray, or even preach and minister by the mind of reason or by the wisdom of God. The works of reason may sound or look impressive, but they accomplish nothing in eternity. The works of those moving by God's wisdom remain forever as an eternal inheritance (1 Corinthians 3:13-15). These two types of "Christian workers," those serving by the mind of reason or those serving by the Spirit, have great difficulty coming into unity. The two sources of thought and direction always strive in contradictions and conflicts. But remember this: the power and glory of God are only manifested on earth in Christians moving by the wisdom of God.

Jesus will separate the sheep and the goats at the end of the age (Matthew 25:32). Some who called Him, "Lord, Lord," never really knew Him. Some who performed seemingly mighty works "in His name" never ministered at His command (Matthew 7:22,23). They ministered out of their own spirits, their own concepts of Christian living, or even under the control of demonic spirits. Others ministered with child-like faith in God's Word, never comprehending the magnitude of their kindness and mercy extended to others. They simply obeyed God's voice in compassion and love. Yet, they are eternally rewarded at Christ's return.

Visions and dreams are "the real"; visualization is "the counterfeit." Peter quoted the prophet, Joel, on the Day of Pentecost by proclaiming, ". . . Your sons and your daughters shall prophesy, your old men shall dream dreams, your young men shall see visions . . ." (Joel 2:28-32; Acts 2:17-21). Joseph was a dreamer who saved his nation from starvation and held a high ranking position in a foreign government (Genesis 37:5; 41:40). Daniel interpreted dreams and received visions of the last days (Daniel 1:17; 2:10-28).

Peter, Paul and John all received visions which directed the early Church. Peter's sermon promised "dreams and visions" on the day of Pentecost, indicating that the indwelling Holy Spirit opens Christians to receive insights from the Lord. Visions and dreams are one way that God communicates with His people. Visions and dreams are especially important to leaders who direct ministries. The pattern in the Word of God verifies, "Surely the Lord God does nothing, unless He reveals His secret to His servants the prophets" (Amos 3:7). Paul prayed for the early Church to receive, ". . . the spirit of wisdom and revelation in the knowledge of Him . . ." (Ephesians 1:17).

The counterfeit of visions and dreams is "visualization" which leads to wicked imaginations. The Tower of Babel is a good example of the power of a wicked imagination. God said concerning the people's evil intentions ". . . nothing that they propose to do will be withheld from them" (Genesis 11:6). The idea for the Tower of Babel was born in pride of achievement as a monument built to honor man. One of the six things the Lord hates is ". . . a heart that devises wicked plans . . ." (Proverbs 6:18).

Paul warned that God's wrath falls mightily on those devising plans with a wicked imagination. He said, ". . . because, although they knew God, they did not glorify Him as God, nor were thankful, but became futile in their thoughts, and their foolish hearts were darkened" (Romans 1:21). Paul also writes, ". . . casting down arguments and every high thing that exalts itself against the knowledge of God, bringing every thought into captivity to the obedience of Christ . . ." (2 Corinthians 10:5).

Any Christian recognizes the danger of wicked imaginations. The mirage of "visualization" associates Eastern mysticism with "the true" visualizing faith. For example, the woman with an issue of blood visualized herself touching the hem of Jesus' garment in order to be healed (Matthew 9:20,21). Were her thoughts motivated by a wicked imagination or faith? Of course, she visualized in faith, acted in faith and received healing virtue from Jesus.

Abraham, the father of the household of faith, was a classic "visualizer." God told him to look at the stars in the sky and "visualize" them as the number of his sons and daughters (Genesis 15:5). What a ridiculous visualization for a man so advanced in years! Yet, the Bible says that Abraham "did not waver at the promise of God through unbelief, but was strengthened in faith . . ." (Romans 4:20).

Fearmongers who warn against "visualization" point to obvious dangers of occult probing and interaction with demonic spirits. But the danger of emphasizing occult "visualization" is that Christians begin to back away from promises of God for their own lives, families and churches.

The concept of "thought forms" are neither good nor evil. Thoughts are good or evil depending upon the source, the underlying motives and the fruit those thoughts yield. People determined to "seek first the Kingdom of God and His righteousness" are not in danger of occult "thought forms" nor of idolatry by visualizing Jesus. Any temptations toward wicked imaginations are obvious to a Spirit-led Christian. The Holy Spirit convicts us immediately, and the power to resist temptation is resident in every child of God.

Satan can kill the one who is a visionary, but he can never kill a vision from God. Joseph's half brothers hated him for his dreams. Spiritual "half brothers" hate dreamers today. Dreamers are not popular with world systems nor with Pharisees. Visionaries are often lonely men and women who face rejection, misunderstanding and accusations from their contemporaries. Their motives are always questioned. They burn with inner fire; therefore, they don't give up even when facing the most perilous tribulation (Matthew 23:35).

Joseph suffered many tribulations during the thirteen years of his slavery, and was imprisoned because of false accusations. Paul was beaten, imprisoned, impoverished and constantly attacked by both Christian and non-Christian leaders. Daniel spent the night in a lion's den for refusing to compromise his prayers. John died in exile on an island, yet as a man totally fulfilled in his calling. Christians have died as martyrs throughout the centuries for their faith. How is such fortitude cultivated? Visionaries and dreamers see the unseen and "know that they know" they have received truth from God. Though they seem foolish to the world, and infuriate their half brothers, they give their lives in faithfulness to heavenly visions which set the course of their destinies and those whom they lead.

Dreamers threaten and challenge the status quo of society and religion. Martin Luther King, Jr. was a twentieth century dreamer who is honored today, but his vision of racial equality which he saw "from the mountain" threatened the social structure of America in the 50's and 60's.

The unity of believers is "the real," contrasting the networking of the New Age which is a "counterfeit." Jesus would have never prayed to God for something impossible or contrary to His will. Jesus prayed, ". . . that they all may be one . . . that the world may believe that You sent Me" (John 17:21). Paul writes that Jesus gave apostles, prophets, evangelists, pastors and teachers to the Church "for the equipping of the saints for the work of ministry, for the edifying of the body of Christ, till we all come to the unity of the faith and the knowledge of the Son of God . . ." (Ephesians 4:11-13). So why are many Christians fearful of unity of faith in the body of Christ?

Many Bible teachers warn that a world leader, the Antichrist, will emerge from a one world religious system. They teach that the scenes recorded in John's Revelation of Jesus Christ are dispensational, future events of history. They warn that any move toward Christian unity will open the door for the Antichrist to take over. Meanwhile, some Christian leaders set goals of unity by the mind of reason in organizational structure. Pseudo-Christian cults, such as the New Age Movement or the Unification Church, promote unity in a one-world religion. They advocate mixing any beliefs "in God" into one, loosely structured conglomerate. No wonder the subject of unity is so controversial among Christians.

Yet, Jesus said, "Father, make them one . . ." Satan wars the fulfillment of that prayer. The witness of unity of faith among Christians will manifest the Kingdom of God "on earth as it is in heaven." I know that statement is strong, but I willingly defend it. Christians will never come into a unity of doctrine, but they must come into a unity of faith based on Jesus Christ, the Son of the living God.

Our confession of Jesus is the "rock" of revelation upon which the Church is built (Matthew 16:17,18). Diversity of doctrine and forms of worship do not make unity impossible. God created diversity as demonstrated in the variety of flowers, trees and all species of natural creation. We must also realize that as members of the body of Christ, we function in diversity of callings in the same body. Not everyone functions as a hand or a foot or an ear, but we are members of Christ's body on earth. Who has the right to say to another member, "I don't need you!"? (1 Corinthians 12).

We must realize that anyone working against unity among Christians is not speaking in the spirit of Christ. Sadly, factions and divisions characterize the Church today. But warnings are appropriate to the one who causes strife among brothers! Only hardened spirits refuse to extend grace to others whose perspectives are not identical! Fearmongers plant suspicion in Christians' hearts concerning efforts to bring a spirit of unity to brothers and sisters in Christ!

The image of Christ in believers is "the real"; self-realization of godhood is "the counterfeit." Man was created in the image of God. Satan, who declared that he would ascend to the throne of the Most High . . . and make himself "like God," has hated man since creation (Isaiah 14:13,14). Why? God's plan to defeat Satan through the Seed of the woman culminated in Jesus Christ's death on the cross and His resurrection from the grave. Now the Church is beginning to wake up to the knowledge that "Christ in us [you], the hope of glory" is Satan's final death blow (Colossians 1:27). No teaching is more threatening to Satan than "Christ in us"! He attacks Christians with fear at claiming their inheritance or demonstrating the resurrection power within us.

Satan accuses Christians of thinking of themselves as being "like gods" because he fears the truth of Christians finding out the meaning of living "in His image." He is as subtle now as he was in the Garden of Eden. One day he puffs us with pride over spiritual victories. The next day we feel defeated and weak against insignificant obstacles to God's will. Many Christians ride a spiritual roller coaster—up one day, tackling mountains, down the next day, ready to give up. Those Christians desiring most to live for the Lord seem either to fly or to crawl. In the Church today, enlightenment into God's Word is bringing balance and true spiritual perception of our responsibility in God's plan.

We are vessels of honor, temples of the Holy Spirit, new creations in Christ, the bride of Christ on earth. We have feet of clay, but we also have the anointed power of Jesus Christ residing within us. We are created in God's image with the responsibility to lift up Jesus for the world to see. Jesus said, ". . . he who believes in Me, the works that I do he will do also; and greater works than these he will do, because I go to My Father" (John 14:12). That power within us doesn't make us great; it makes Him great!

Jesus called us to be the "light of the world" and the "salt of the earth" (Matthew 5:13,14). Light lends visibility and direction. Salt permeates and flavors society. Of course Satan wars such a revolutionizing identity. He accuses, threatens and intimidates our boldness. The more bold and effective a ministry becomes, the more Satan accuses that ministry of trying to be "like God." Satan attacks credibility and minimizes the evidence of God's anointing in lasting fruit. Front-line ministries moving with the greatest measure of faith and anointing from God receive the harshest criticism and attacks.

No man is wise to trust the flesh of another person. But Christians must begin to recognize and trust "the Christ" in their covenant brothers. If we truly believe that He makes us into new creations, why emphasize our lack of spirituality to insure that we remain humble? How easily we recognize our weaknesses. Paul said he would rather boast in his infirmities [weaknesses] that the power of Christ might rest upon him (2 Corinthians 12:9).

We need to edify the Christ-nature within us to grow, stretch and press forward in the Spirit. We can do all things through Christ who strengthens us (Philippians 4:13). What does exhortation and edification really mean? Of course, we guard against pride, self-aggrandizement and focusing on personalities in ministry. But God effectively chastens His children Himself (Hebrews 12:6,7). God will share His glory with no man, yet He chooses to manifest Himself to the world through human vessels.

True prophets are "the real"; false prophets are "the counterfeit." The Church is built on the foundation of apostles and prophets. Jesus Christ is the Chief Cornerstone (Ephesians 2:20). The ministries of teachers, pastors and evangelists have been readily received by the modern Church. But without the ministry of apostles and prophets, the Church has lacked wisdom and authority. The resulting powerlessness, lack of direction and fragmentation are obvious. Society easily ignores the influence of the Church today. They hear numerous, conflicting voices saying, "Here is the Christ." The trumpet has an uncertain sound.

Prophetic ministries give direction from God. The Church is the prophetic army that Ezekiel saw in a vision. Dry bones lay in a valley. God asked Ezekiel, "Son of man, can these bones live?" Then God commanded Ezekiel to prophesy over those bones saying, "O dry bones, hear the word of the Lord!" As Ezekiel prophesied, the bones came alive and stood as an exceedingly great army (Ezekiel 37:1-14). Who are the generals in God's army today?

The Church is disorganized and unprepared for warfare. Christians don't know how to use spiritual weapons effectively. Lines of spiritual authority are vague or ignored. Lack of spiritual headship leaves homes in shambles. The Church follows behind society's chaos, cleaning up the mess. Instead we should be leading the way in social values, demonstrating a standard of abundant living. Only prophetic voices, anointed of God, can make dry bones live.

Jesus said that false prophets would characterize the last days. False prophets, soothsayers, weather prophets often move in the same circles as anointed prophets of the Lord. They "tickle the ears" of people, saying the things people want to hear. That is not to say that they necessarily bring good news. Often their message is gloom and doom.

False prophets use negative reports to make people feel good about themselves. People justify their own spiritual shortcomings by comparing themselves with corruption abounding everywhere! Instead of being set free from bondage or feeling challenged to grow spiritually, people just want to "hang on 'til Jesus comes." False prophets use fear tactics to control people. Even righteous living is prompted by fear. Discipline of the flesh characterizes spirituality rather than responding to the goodness of God in a loving relationship with Him.

False prophets prophesy out of their own spirits or by spirits of divination. They interpret Scripture to fit world events. True prophets unfold fresh insights into the Scriptures. The mysteries of God's Word become reality as they are understood by the interpretation of the Holy Spirit.

When a true prophet speaks, choices must be made. Even "hard sayings" call for choices that lead to either life or death. Jesus said:

> ". . . unless you eat the flesh of the Son of Man and drink His blood, you have no life in you" . . . Therefore many of His disciples, when they heard this, said, "This is a hard saying; who can understand it?" . . . Jesus said, "The words that I speak to you are spirit, and they are life. But there are some of you who do not believe." For Jesus knew from the beginning who they were who did not believe, and who would betray Him. And He said, "Therefore I have said to you that no one can come to Me unless it has been granted to him by My Father." From that time many of His disciples went back and walked with Him no more. (John 6:53,60,63-66)

The fruit of a true prophetic ministry are people who live and move in confidence—righteousness, peace and joy in the Holy Spirit. The fruit of a false prophetic ministry are people who live and move in defensiveness, fear and negative expectations of the future.

The new birth is "the real"; rebirthing is "the counterfeit." An area of ministry under tremendous attack today is the area of Christian counseling. I believe that the root of this controversy is Satan's fear of God's people becoming emotionally well and strong. The world has viewed Christians as emotional cripples using Jesus as a "crutch" to endure the pain of life. Karl Marx called religion "an opiate of the people." Sadly, the lives of many genuine, born-again Christians substantiate Marx's view rather than challenge it. When Christians focus on their needs, they hinder the witness of Jesus Christ's overcoming power. The new birth allows us the see the Kingdom of God (John 3:3).

Unless we enter the Kingdom with the demonstration of the gospel that Jesus taught and lived, we remain spiritual infants. The state of infancy is not a very attractive way to live. Others must keep us clean and constantly care for us. Maturity and responsibility increase as we grow in understanding. Natural and spiritual growth parallel one another in concept, except that time is not the major factor in spiritual growth. Spiritual growth depends upon one's inner desire and openness to the Holy Spirit's direction. Time is important in spiritual growth to solidify our faith to move at God's command. In this regard, seasoning and experience are far more important than age in determining spiritual maturity.

The controversy in the Church over inner healing and rebirthing divert attention away from the new birth in Jesus Christ. Fearmongers have purposely associated psychological counseling with occult practices. They alert Christians to the danger of mental images of Jesus, calling such images "idols." They warn that rebirthing, a counseling procedure promoted by Agnes Sanford of imagining oneself in the womb to deal with deep-seated trauma in one's life, grows out of shamanistic cult healing (Hunt, p.124-131). Let me firmly state that I do not endorse these techniques, nor do I practice them in my counseling ministry. However, I am convinced that criticism of rebirthing and inner healing has been exploitative and overstated. The warning plants fear of Christian counseling in the hearts of Christians who desperately need help.

Spiritual counseling and discernment are "the real"; mind control is "the counterfeit." The mark of spiritual maturity is discernment. Discernment is the greatest need in the body of Christ today. The entire New Testament was written to Christians —people who are born again and filled with the Spirit of God—who still had problems after they were saved. Many Christians bring scars, wounds, emotional barriers and pain with them into their "new life" in Jesus Christ. Sanctification is a process. The parable of the sower sowing the Word shows how weeds and lack of good soil can even destroy the potential harvest (Mark 4:1-9). The spiritual laws of sowing and reaping apply to born again believers, affecting their emotions, concepts, conduct and spiritual growth.

Psychology is a study of the "psyche" or working of the mind, emotions and human behavior. Like theology (the study of God) or sociology (the study of society), the study itself is neither good nor evil. The integrity and skill of the counselors determine the improper or proper use of psychological information. The Bible encourages man to learn God's laws and principles from nature. Paul asks, "Does not even nature itself teach you . . ." (1 Corinthians 11:14). The writer of Proverbs says, "Go to the ant, you sluggard! Consider her ways and be wise . . ." (Proverbs 6:6).

I do not believe that someone becomes a "Christian psychologist" any more than a "Christian auto mechanic." But Christians can be psychologists or auto mechanics, or they can work in other professions. I disagree totally with those promoting fear of psychologists as if they practice voodoo or black magic.

I suggest that critics of psychology consider the state of society if all mental hospitals were suddenly closed. Where would people go who are now treated in mental hospitals? Many mentally ill people are confined for their own sakes as well as the sake of their families and society. Imagine losing the wealth of research we have accumulated to recognize and treat certain mental disorders. Psychological research has benefited medicine, law enforcement and educational programs for the mentally and emotionally impaired. Should we also throw out the practice of medicine because some medical researchers and doctors are unbelievers, or because witchdoctors practice healing rites in pagan societies?

Jesus is described prophetically by Isaiah as the "Counselor" (Isaiah 9:6). Jesus called the Holy Spirit our "Counselor or Helper" (John 15:26). Jesus Himself exemplified a counselor. For example, while visiting Mary and Martha, He addressed Martha's anxiety and critical reprimand that her sister did not help her prepare the meal (Luke 10:41,42). Solomon is regarded as a mighty counselor through the gift of wisdom which God gave to Him (1 Kings 4:29). Paul includes the gifts of wisdom, knowledge and discernment of spirits as ministry gifts in the Church (1 Corinthians 12:8-11).

Counseling and spiritual discernment bring life and inner freedom to a Christian, whereas mind control results in emotional dependency and bondage. Many cults physically close people away from their families, society or any influences the religious leaders cannot monitor. This isolation aids in using techniques of mind control. Christian counseling builds up believers in faith, while mind control destroys personal confidence and identity. The goal of a Christian counselor is to foster maturity and wholeness in one seeking help—to bring one to the renewal of his mind in Jesus Christ (Romans 12:2).

Mind control keeps people immature and unable to discern truth. They live in fear of error. They are afraid to move in faith because they go to the church with a "give me" orientation rather than a "send me" confidence. Mind control breeds spiritual parasites who take from ministry rather than give their lives in service to the Lord.

Miracles of God are "the real"; lying wonders are "the counterfeit." It's interesting to note that some critics of Christian ministries belong to churches which do not teach or believe that miracles are for today. Ministries they attack, for the most part, are ones who teach that the power of God is available in our generation. I am certain that we stand on the horizon of renewed apostolic power in the Church at the greatest dimension in history.

Miracles, signs and wonders threaten powers of darkness because they draw so much attention to the message of Jesus Christ. Satan uses two counter tactics. First, he wants people either to fear or ridicule miracles in skepticism. He plants enough charlatans to discredit true testimonies of God's miracle working power. Along with that strategy, Satan also performs his own miracles. Pharaoh's magicians (Exodus 8:18,19); Elymas, a magician whom Paul cursed with blindness (Acts 13:8-11); and Simon, the sorcerer (Acts 8:9), all were used by Satan to divert attention from God's miracle-working power. Praise God, each one failed in confrontation with "the real"!

The millennium reign of Christ is "the real"; the New Age Movement's New World is "the counterfeit." I am eager to discuss the New Age Movement because their teaching, goals and strategy are powerfully deceptive. Even their language is close to—and often exactly like—"the real." I am reminded that the Word of God says Satan is "like a roaring lion" (1 Peter 5:8), but Jesus is "the Lion of Judah" (Revelation 5:5). The New Agers talk "unity, brotherhood and peace" as well as a "new world" that paints an attractive picture of utopia.

Meanwhile, Christians long for the reign of Christ on earth. They eagerly await the reconciliation of all things, when "the wolf also shall dwell with the lamb, the leopard shall lie down with the young goat, the calf and the young lion and the fatling together; and a little child shall lead them" (Isaiah 11:6). What's the difference in the two? Many things, but they can be summarized in one debate: the spirit of humanism versus the power of the Holy Spirit.

Man will never, never achieve unity, peace or perfection by his own efforts. Never! The mind of reason plots ways that "seem right to a man, but its end is the way of death" (Proverbs 14:12). Humanism is an antichrist spirit which John said, ". . . is now already in the world" (1 John 4:3). Why antichrist? If man can save, sanctify and redeem the world himself, he does not need a Savior, the Christ, to redeem him. Humanism negates the work of the cross in our lives. Humanists set their minds to build the Tower of Babel all over again.

The danger of the New Age Movement is all their good-sounding goals. They appeal to our pride in the most deceptive way because they are "cause" oriented. People today are looking for a cause worthy of their lives. Sadly, the Church has been asleep. We've sung about "heaven" and let the world go to hell.

Jesus' gospel was totally "cause" oriented. He preached "the Kingdom of heaven is at hand" (Matthew 4:17). Pilate asked Jesus if He were a King and He answered, "It is as you say" (Mark 15:2). Isaiah said that the governments [of the world] would be upon His shoulders (Isaiah 9:6). Herod sought to kill the babe born in Bethlehem because His kingship threatened the Roman government. Jesus is the King of a real Kingdom! The mature Church is preparing, waiting aggressively for the coming of the Bride-groom to rule and reign. And the bride is growing up quickly.

The round rainbow as a sign of covenant with God is "the real"; the New Age rainbow symbol is "the counterfeit." A spiritual "counterfeit" usually precedes "the real." The mirage rises to divert attention from a genuine move of God. An example from my own ministry at Chapel Hill Harvester Church in Atlanta is a classic case. In 1982, I had a vision of the throne of God which changed my ministry. I shared the vision with my congregation. From the teaching that followed that vision, I wrote a book called *Ultimate Kingdom*. The people in my congregation came into a new understanding of covenant with God and their calling to demonstrate responsible Christianity.

As a church, we wore pins of the round rainbow which I saw in the vision of God's throne. The center of the rainbow was a "K," standing for the Kingdom of God. I explained to the people that the top of the rainbow represented God's covenant with us, and the bottom half stood for our covenant with Him.

Shortly after we began wearing our "K-pins," a book was written on the dangers of cults, focusing on the symbol of the round rainbow. Suddenly, the beautiful covenant relationship with the Lord, to which thousands of people had committed, was suspected of association with a cult because we wore a symbol of covenant. Some were calling our church "a cult." The members of the Presbytery at our church discussed several times whether we should stop wearing the pins. I remained firm. The rainbow is God's idea— not the devil's! Why should God's people back away from something that God gives to us because the devil builds a look-alike mirage to scare us away?

I'm sure Satan thought he was really smart to give "the rainbow" to the New Agers. One of the major revelations to the body of Christ today is the impor- tance of covenant with God. Christians will never endure the testings of the last days without activat- ing their covenant of protection "under the shadow of the Almighty" (Psalm 91). Jesus said, ". . . as the days of Noah were, so also will the coming of the Son of Man be" (Matthew 24:37). How shrewd to associate the sign of God's covenant promise to man with a pseudo-Christian movement.

Do we run in fear of a mirage? Do we back away and let Satan win? No! We pray for discernment. We hold fast to that which is true. We expose and unmask Satan. And through the fire of revelation, we destroy any attempts to promote "the counterfeit" or to foster fear of "the real" source of our help.

4

THE POSITIVE & NEGATIVE ASPECTS OF CHURCH CONTROVERSY

Discerning of spirits is of God. An inquirer mentality is satanic. I'm reminded of that advertisement on television where the announcer asks, "Who wants to know?" People glare into the camera answering, "I want to know!" Are these readers who "want to know" merely seeking truth? What are the benefits of their "knowing" controversial details of famous people's lives? What are the reporters' motives in collecting information for these publications?

Some teachers in these last days cater to people who perceive themselves to be "spiritual," but listen to gospel sermons with "itching ears." Immature Christians enjoy sensationalism, accusations, gossip, quotes taken out of context or misquoted, and public exposure of any weaknesses—true or fabricated—in Christian ministries. They revel in statistics on the sad state of society and failures in the Christian community. They enjoy details describing the sorrows of others. Sadly, the Church is currently bombarded with spiritual smut in the media. Too many Christian broadcasts and publications are filled with spicy tidbits of information, proclaimed with the merchandising motives of tabloid journalists!

What a tragedy! The Church suffers needlessly from such immaturity. Instead, we should be focusing on proclaiming the good news of Christ's Kingdom. The instruments of diversionary tactics, no matter how well-meaning they are, must answer to God. Too few Christians possess a solid scriptural foundation strong enough to weather controversy among Church leadership. "Little ones" become the spiritual casualties of internal war in the Church. Many Christians today are experiencing painful, and sometimes fatal disillusionment toward their leaders. God's Kingdom is built in trust. Sheep need to have trustworthy shepherds who minister with an understanding of both the rewards and consequences of their accountability to God.

Amid controversy, many signs indicate that the Church is growing up in our generation. The mature bride of Christ will not be "tossed to and fro and carried about with every wind of doctrine, by the trickery of men, in the cunning craftiness by which they lie in wait to deceive . . ." (Ephesians 4:14). The time has come for the Church to "put away childish things" (1 Corinthians 13:11). I pray that the Holy Spirit will use the widespread focus on issues Dave Hunt raises to open our eyes to greater understanding. God will cause His bride to mature using the same controversy which Satan intended to separate and destroy our witness. God uses struggles in warfare to teach His bride discernment.

What are the benefits derived from an ecclesiastical tug-of-war? Solutions are not usually found in our debates. We must not use carnal weapons in spiritual conflicts. Warfare begins in the heavenly realm. Intercession is an aggressive force in spiritual combat and in preparation to face any circumstance of life. God's Word assures us that whenever Satan's forces come in like a flood, God raises a standard. "So shall they fear the name of the Lord from the west, and His glory from the rising of the sun; when the enemy comes in like a flood, the Spirit of the Lord will lift up a standard against him" (Isaiah 59:19).

The standard of God shines through His people today like never before. God's standard is the witness of Christian men and women who live in covenant with God, understanding their responsibility in their generation. Their witness demonstrates a lifestyle of God's grace, power and excellence. The Kingdom of God within believers—righteousness, peace and joy in the Holy Spirit—is manifested in the visible domain of this world as committed Christians live out "His Kingdom on earth as it is in heaven." Finally, Jesus Christ Himself will return to rule and reign on earth with His mature bride, the glorious Church.

A victorious outcome to this warfare is promised to God's people who endure to the end. To encourage overcoming Christians, allow me to offer five positive and five negative aspects of controversy in the Church today. First, let's examine the positive aspects of controversy:

1. **Christians are intently examining the dangers of deception which Jesus assured us would characterize the last days.** The call to "test the spirits" has made believers more discerning. Christian teachers speak more carefully, weighing the impact of their influence and rightly handling the Word of truth. The need for discernment against error has opened the spirits of people to rely on the Holy Spirit, their Helper and Guide, as well as the counsel of elders in the body of Christ. Discernment of spirits is never derived by research or factual, statistical knowledge. Christians filled with the Holy Spirit reject error in teaching by sensitivity to the inner promptings or warnings of the Holy Spirit.

2. **Christian theologians and teachers have been forced into examining scriptural truth.** I have received requests from numerous Church leaders recently who ask if they can schedule time for dialogue with me on various Church doctrines. I thank God continually for the dedication to truth that I find motivating men and women of God today. They diligently seek answers by searching the Scriptures.

Many teachers submit their questions to extensive counsel of eldership in the body of Christ. They are not content merely to recite "high sounding" phrases or rely on teaching based on their denominational traditions. They want workable answers. The gospel of Jesus Christ must be both communicated and demonstrated in the lives of His people. God's direction becomes applicable in practical solutions to remedy the chaos of our society.

3. **Christians of diverse doctrines and beliefs are entering into dialogue and vulnerable communication with one another.** Walls are

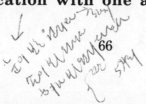

crumbling. I think that's great! God has allowed this focus on deception and controversy to close the ranks of His people against our true enemy, Satan and his cohorts. God's army is like the dry bones which came together as Ezekiel prophesied over them (Ezekiel 37:3-5).

We are discovering that our similarities outweigh our differences. We may function differently and fight in diverse divisions of the army, but we're on the winning side in the same war. Christians are finally talking as well as listening to one another. We're asking, "What is God really saying to His people today?" As Christian eldership flow in their callings in the five-fold ministry, God's people find safety. The Church serves as a fortress and refuge, a place of restoration from life's storms. We're raising standards against the onslaught of confusion unleashed by the devil to kill, steal and destroy lives.

4. **Various Church doctrines must now be examined according to the historical theology of the Church and the harmony of Scriptures.** Line upon line, precept upon precept, God is bringing His Church into anointed demonstration of His Word. This understanding rests on the foundation laid by the apostles and prophets that has survived throughout the centuries. Jesus is the Cornerstone, and the apostles and prophets laid the foundation on which the Church is built (Ephesians 2:20). We build confidently, recognizing the interaction of the Holy Spirit with God's covenant people from the first century Church to our present day. True enlightenment of God's Word always brings us to an historical consensus that exposes counterfeit doctrines which do not endure the test of time. Counterfeit theories fall during the historical tests of spiritual warfare. Theo-

logical theories alone have no power nor enduring fruit.

For example, years ago many preachers from the South "proved" scripturally that racial segregation was God's will. Some preachers were so deceived that they taught that black people were born under an ancient curse. They pointed to scripture, justifying their own racial prejudices by saying that Ham was cursed to be a black man because he looked at the nakedness of his father, Noah. They reasoned that Ham's sin cursed an entire race of people. Such "Bible teaching" justified their prejudices against blacks living in the twentieth century. Of course, that lie was born out of hell! In the first place, racial diversity began at the Tower of Babel. The point I wish to emphasize is that true enlightenment of the Holy Spirit always exposes biblical error and sets God's people free to reach their full potential in Him.

Today some preachers still "prove" that the harlot church is the Roman Catholic Church. How tragic that these preachers have closed themselves off from sharing warm fellowship in Jesus Christ with beautiful born-again Catholic brothers and sisters. The Holy Spirit is exposing the true harlot church. She is a self-serving religious system, engrossed in worldly pursuits and controlled by mammon's strongholds.

How is the harlot church exposed? By contrasting her selfish values with the self-sacrifice of the true bride of Christ. The true bride always embraces God's strategy of the cross. The true bride dies to self-interests as she ministers God's will in resurrection power. The "salt" and "light" of society lift up the name of Jesus in their daily lifestyles and life choices. Their witness to the world proclaims that Jesus is Lord over their circumstances. They seek first His

Kingdom, not their own interests.

Instead of "proving" or "justifying" self-serving beliefs, I am excited that Christians are dedicated to becoming living demonstrations of the central message of the Bible. The Bible unfolds a story of restoration for all mankind. In the beginning, the Spirit moved across a world that was without form and void. God moved across the face of this planet to correct rebellion in the universe.

Now men and women of God are taking seriously their commission to correct destructive forces gripping our world. Empowered by the Holy Spirit, we are taking dominion over evil. Though Adam and Eve failed in obedience to God, He promised that the Seed of the woman would bring total victory over Satan. Restoration of "that which was lost" is the central theme of the Bible. Abraham's example of faith and covenant with God, Jesus Christ's teaching concerning the gospel of the Kingdom and the meaning of His redemption of all creation on the cross, the purpose of God's sending of the Holy Spirit at Pentecost—all these truths make some of our debates seem rather lifeless by contrast. Much of the controversy in the Church today is a mirage diverting our attention from the real concerns of God's heart.

Based on the historical theological debates of the Church, an examination of contemporary controversy is a positive factor. Bear with me in my folly, but I'm amused that many critics of ministries today never studied in seminaries or Bible colleges. Today many laymen who have never received any formal biblical scholarship to their credit are attempting to be theologians or critics of ministries. They are turning their opinions on religion into writing careers at the expense of readers who are seeking truth for their lives.

One of my concerns over these writers' lack of formal scholarship is that Sunday School classes are being taught from their books. These authors lack valid credentials not only educationally, but more importantly, as bearers of spiritual fruit in the same kind of work as the ministries they criticize. A reader must ask, "What is the author's fruit in this kind of ministry?" Spiritual fruit either confirms or refutes the anointing of God.

Historically, God has moved through His called-out five-fold ministry—those who must give account for the care of souls (Hebrews 13:17). I pray that people will realize it is only when they stay within the framework of God's structure—submission to the direction of the five-fold ministry—that maturity comes. When people outside of God's structure of authority move as self-appointed judges or critics of ministries, they not only cause confusion in the body of Christ, but they open themselves to God's judgment. David recognized God's structure of authority when he said, "The Lord forbid that I should do this thing to my master [Saul], the Lord's anointed, to stretch out my hand against him, seeing he is the anointed of the Lord ... Therefore let the Lord be judge ..." (1 Samuel 24:4,15).

5. **The Church is forced to her knees to pray for discernment and guidance to truth.** As I previously stated, men and women of God are seeking His direction with greater intensity today. The Church finds the true mind of God on her knees in prayer. God searches for people who hunger and thirst to know Him and share His heart! As people knock, seek, search and press for answers, God will hear from heaven. He always responds to those seek-

ing Him. God delivers His people from bondage and error when they cry out to Him for answers. Confusion ends when we turn to God with our hearts, humbly asking, "Lead us not into temptation, but deliver us from evil . . ."

Now, let's examine some of the negative aspects of controversy in the Church:

1. **Controversy always surfaces new reasons for division in the body of Christ.** Sowing contention is a sin against God. It is one act which the Bible plainly states that "God hates" (Proverbs 6:16-19). Jesus prayed, "Father make them one." Any teacher or writer who purposely plants seeds of division among Christians today must examine his motives very carefully. Satan works to "divide and conquer" the army of the Lord. Spiritual unity always accomplishes God's purposes. Jesus said that when we agree "as touching anything, it shall be done . . ."

I was signing one of my books recently at a convention when a man approached me with a wild look in his eyes. The first question he asked me was, "Whose camp are you in?" I smiled and replied, "I am in Jesus' camp!" Honestly, I didn't know there was any other camp to consider!

He ignored my reply and continued, "I mean, are you in Dave Hunt's or Hal Lindsey's camp? Or do you belong to the camp of Robert Schuller, Paul Cho, or Earl Paulk?"

I looked at him and said, "I am Earl Paulk." He almost fainted!

Are Christians identifying themselves by "camps"? Hasn't the time finally come to identify ourselves as born-again, Spirit-filled Christians rather than wearing some label, or even worse, a teacher's name? Why not live under Jesus' name! God only sees two camps:

the kingdom of darkness and the Kingdom of light. I know some teachers disagree with me on this, but I am certain that Christ cannot return to earth until His Church is joined in spiritual unity of faith (1 Thessalonians 5:4). Who would He come back to receive as His bride? The Baptists? The Methodists? The Pentecostals?

Scripture indicates that Christ will return for those who are prepared for Him, waiting aggressively in obedience to God. We are in preparation as we follow the Holy Spirit's guidance. How sad that we allow division in the Church to rob us of focusing on our preparation for the coming of the King. Controversy diverts us from the main thrust of demonstrating the gospel of Christ to powers and principalities and bringing salvation to a dying world. Controversy delays the fulfillment of God's plan.

2. **Controversy in the Church is flaunted before the eyes of an unbelieving world.** The Apostle Paul confronted this problem in the early church by asking, "How dare you go to the courts of the world to settle your disputes?" (1 Corinthians 6:1). "Don't you know that you are going to judge angels?" (1 Corinthians 6:3). Genuine correction under God's guidelines stipulated in Scripture requires that an offense first be addressed face to face between disputing parties. We must make an effort to come to peaceful resolutions without defiling others (2 Timothy 2:23-26). I can personally testify to the omission of any opportunities to explain scriptural stands I have taken, or to defend statements I have written that were quoted in Dave Hunt's book. I can only speculate on the reasons for published "correction" of my teaching.

I have been preaching the gospel of Jesus Christ

for forty-two years. In one of my books, *Satan Unmasked*, I emphasized that man was created in God's image. I wholeheartedly believe that "Christ in us is the hope of glory" (Colossians 1:27). Either one believes that man is created in the image of God, or he believes in the evolution of man from a lower species of life. In keeping with the Genesis account of creation in which each "kind produce their own kind," I wrote, "Just as dogs have puppies and cats have kittens, God has little gods."

That one statement quoted by Dave Hunt in *Seduction of Christianity* thrust me into a category with others accused of teaching humanism, rebellion against God, and "seduction" of believers into a cult mentality! Out of context, perhaps I would have questioned the theological validity of the quote. At least, I would have asked for further development of the analogy. I do teach a difference between man seeking to be "like God" which is sin, and being created in the "image of God" which is the essence of man's redemption through Jesus Christ.

Let me state openly that I have never received one telephone call, one letter, one telegram, or one message initiated by Dave Hunt. To neglect giving me the opportunity to defend my statement, quoted in his book as an example of apostasy, is poor journalistic judgment at best. At its worst, I speak only for myself in saying that Dave Hunt neglected to follow instructions written in God's Word in dealing with his "offense" at my teaching.

One of America's leading evangelists, who endorses *Seduction of Christianity* and has invited Dave Hunt to be his guest several times, stated on national television that God intends for His people to be "little Jesuses" doing the work of the ministry in the world.

I shouted, "Amen!" Immediately, I could have wept at realizing that the Church bickers and divides over semantics when we should be united in our witness. What a tragedy! We say the same things differently. Then we accuse one another of teaching error. Meanwhile, the world looks on in confusion, concluding that no one really has the answers to life's critical questions.

3. **The attention of the Church has been focused on the counterfeit—beliefs and practices of the occult—rather than on the gospel of Jesus Christ, the only hope for mankind and the future of the world.** Christians invest time and resources studying "evil" instead of giving their energy in pursuit of godly causes that lift up the name of Jesus. A "counterfeit" always indicates that the "real" exists somewhere. Discernment separates "the precious" from "the worthless." Books written on exposing ministries believed to be counterfeits hardly bring edification to Christians. What is the fruit of such probing? Suspicion. Fear. Doubt. Insecurity and mistrust of spiritual leadership. Could the source of teaching producing this fruit be from God? James answers that question:

> *But the wisdom that is from above is first pure, then peaceable, gentle, willing to yield, full of mercy and good fruits, without partiality and without hypocrisy. Now the fruit of righteousness is sown in peace by those who make peace. (James 3:17,18)*

Daily, repeatedly, I dedicate my ministry to proclaiming the good news of the Kingdom of God! I want to speak boldly the wisdom from above, offending only those who oppose God's purposes in the earth! Jesus Christ, love, faith, hope, mercy, peace, goodness, gentleness, self-control, restoration, healing, abundant life—this is my message, my focus, my goal in daily demonstration.

Paul warned us to "redeem the time, because the days are evil" (Ephesians 5:15,16). That warning does not exhort us to focus on the evil around us, but to witness boldly to the truth! Anyone can criticize others. Any writer can dedicate himself to pointing out failures and mistakes. No Christian would escape the magnifying glass of someone's dedicated scrutiny of human actions. All flesh falls short of the glory of God. But who among us dedicates himself to lifting high the reality of Christ within us? Who exhorts us to live as standards of righteousness through the power of Christ? Who dedicates himself to peace and unity among God's people? Some teachers devote more effort on teaching about "false prophets" than "true prophets." Some teach about "false prophets" who do not even believe that true prophets speak God's direction in our day. Some teachers emphasize the suffering of the end times more than the glory of God rising upon His people.

4. **The Church is diverted from its primary mission.** Instead of teaching the good news of the Kingdom, we join in a "witch-hunt," searching out seducing spirits and accusing those with whom we disagree. We need to concentrate our efforts more on sharing the good news. Our primary concern needs to be on spiritual birth and growth of people around us. If our efforts focus on edification of believers, we don't have to worry about Christians being deceived. When our minds are filled continually with the good news of God's Word and praises to Him, we recognize opposing spirits easily. Our sensitivity is keen to both good and evil. Discernment is not hidden for one who maintains close fellowship with the Lord.

⑤ **We have turned our attention away from the real enemy to fight against flesh and blood.** Christians, even ministries called of God, war one another instead of our arch foe, Satan. We wrestle against each other with words, alliances and influence rather than wrestling against powers and principalities with spiritual weapons. Our enemies are no longer spiritual forces such as atheism, lawlessness, mammon and humanism. Instead we rage at pastors and churches as if they were enemies opposing God.

Of course, I do not agree totally with every other born-again Christian. I'm sure I never will until Jesus comes. But I do recognize my true enemy! The opposition is clearly identified in Scripture. Satan confronted Jesus directly in person as well as through the accusations of others throughout His ministry. But Jesus always offered people opposing Him the choice of truth or error.

Paul was a great persecutor of the Church until He met Jesus Christ on the road to Damascus. Even with such a jolting encounter with Christ as Paul experienced, Jesus offered him a choice. People in deception are bound by spiritual strongholds. They are always religious and sincere people. These people are not enemies; the strongholds of deception are! Our warfare is not carnal, though the controversy in the Church today attempts to convince us to maintain a tug-of-war in verbal debate. Only the anointing power of God breaks the yoke of bondage—and some strongholds break only by prayer and fasting.

Suppose a history book was written to discuss the lives of influential Americans. The first American this book discusses is Benedict Arnold and his influence. What would be the impression that a reader might surmise of the names to follow? Suppose a book was written to discuss influential personalities in the Bible. This book begins by noting the influence of Judas Iscariot. What expectations would the reader immediately begin to perceive of the author's intentions?

Dave Hunt's book is aimed at "correction" of occult infiltration into Christianity. In the second paragraph of his *Introduction,* he names Jim Jones, the leader of the most devastating mass suicide of our century. By the time the reader finishes the book, the author's intentions seem evident. The reader inevitably associates known cults and false teachers with others whom Dave Hunt quotes.

The Church stands upon the horizon of the most important decades in history. Our opportunity for communicating the witness of Christ is unlimited. Our responsibility before God in the great harvest of these days is critical. Doesn't it seem futile to focus on a mirage of diversion? Why invest our energy on suspicion of one another when God is directing His people in bold demonstration of His Kingdom? Pray for the ears of the Church to be open! Pray for the eyes of our understanding to perceive truth with spiritual vision!

5

PRINCIPLES OF INTERPRETATION

A Christian's biblical perspective will determine his response in theological controversy. Warnings against certain ministries have little effect on Christians who have experienced God's miraculous, anointed power and love in churches consistently teaching principles of the Kingdom of God. Some members of these churches would take the time to discuss the serious implications of scare tactics with those who warn them to beware. I believe most Spirit-filled Christians would simply reply to critics, as the blind man healed by Jesus, ". . . One thing I know: that though I was blind, now I see" (John 9:25).

Consider the perspective of one called "an expert in

cults." This expert dedicates himself to investigating "questionable ministries" in order to expose their flaws. He closely scrutinizes the words of Christian preachers. He hears their tapes, watches their programs on television or reads their books while filtering every word they say through his mental files of research on occult beliefs. He associates all the contemporary examples, vocabulary and applications of Scripture passages these teachers use by comparing their messages with groups he knows teach error. He sits in front of his television, taking notes. He underlines possible quotes he can use in his own books exposing "new" cults. He waits eagerly for some mistake, hoping for more substantial proof to support his suspicions. "Ah! Yes! At last! Another one added to the growing list of influential ministers who are dangerous to Christianity!" He can hardly wait to publish the list of names.

This "expert on cults" is like one who dedicates his life to examining counterfeit bills so that he can compare them to real money. The way experts actually identify counterfeit dollars, quickly recognizing imitations, is by studying the real thing—not the other way around! We do not study error to recognize truth; we study truth to expose error. A person's perspective opens the door of his understanding to truth or deception.

The influence of such witch-hunting zealots is sometimes shortened. Jesus asked Saul of Tarsus, "Saul, Saul, why are you persecuting Me?" (Acts 9:4). I don't question Saul's sincerity in joining the persecution against those enthusiastic, messianic Christians. They were causing problems in the synagogues, attracting crowds with their miracles and upsetting the peaceful social order. Saul believed he was serving God by putting an end to the "rebellion" of these Jewish fanatics. He contended with those who preached that "Jesus Christ has risen from the dead, empowers His followers to minister as He did, and will come again to rule as King of kings and Lord of lords." Saul was a well educated, dedicated Jew. He acted in doing what he believed to be right . . .

Like the blinding light from heaven surrounding Saul, the revelation of God will purge all deception by fire. No one stands against God's will for very long, though God's messengers may be killed or destroyed themselves. Saul watched an angry mob stone Stephen who preached an anointed sermon as he fell to the ground (Acts 7:59,60). Stephen died as a martyr, but his vision, ". . . the heavens opened and the Son of Man standing at the right hand of God" lives on today (Acts 7:56).

Because one's biblical perspective and spiritual experiences are such key factors in discerning truth or error, I must address numerous biblical presuppositions on which critics of ministries build their arguments. First, however, allow me to share principles of interpretation of the Bible which open the Church to deeper insights into God's purposes for us in our generation.

As the Church grows in spiritual maturity, the importance of on-going insights into God's Word are paramount. The word "revelation" should not frighten Christians. The word simply means "to uncover." I am concerned that some Christians object at hearing someone suggest that God continues to speak direction to His Church. God gives direction to all His people today for situations in their lives just as He did in days recorded in the Bible. Seeking deeper understanding of Scripture makes all the difference in a Christian's potential for spiritual growth. I do not intend to apply scriptural interpretations of God's Word in order to disprove others, as some critics of ministries do. Instead, I wish to address principles of biblical interpretation merely to clarify my perspective and to point Christians in a positive direction in understanding God's Word.

A person can interpret any book of the Bible, including visions recorded in the book of Revelation, with a legalistic approach which will make sense. Events of the past and future are linked up and charted . . . one, two, three. That approach represents a legalistic interpretation of God's Word which is the direction many contemporary Bible studies take. This does not mean that the majority of Bible courses and commentaries are necessarily in error in their approach. Most commentaries record the level of understanding that was available to Christian teachers for particular periods of Church history.

The truth in God's Word never changes nor ends. Truth never contradicts itself. Enlightenment of the Holy Spirit continually opens God's people to new comprehension of His ways. The Holy Spirit directs our actions in obedience to Him. Without seeing the full scope of God's plan revealed by the Holy Spirit, many scriptural interpretations in evangelical circles facilitated doctrines of legalism. Arguments separate Christians over such concepts as who "the 144,000" are and what "the beasts and heads" recorded in the Revelation of Jesus Christ represent.

An approach to studying Scripture by the Holy Spirit's enlightenment supersedes legalist interpretations. I realize that statement is difficult for the natural mind to comprehend. But does the Holy Spirit really "lead us into all truth"? Where is the Church today in manifesting the witness of God's Kingdom and authority on this earth? Before we can answer these questions, we must understand principles of interpretation. I list seven principles for interpreting the Word of God which open Christians to the spirit of wisdom and revelation.

Principle number one: **The Word of God was written under inspiration of the Holy Spirit and can be understood only by revelation of the Holy Spirit.** Many people attempt to make the Bible into a book of science, history, poetry, eschatology, or moral laws. It is true that both prose and poetry are contained in God's Word. However, the literary and cultural merit of Scripture, as taught in many colleges and universities, is not the purpose of the book. The Bible was written by "holy men of old, as they were moved upon by the Holy Spirit." While the Holy Spirit used the hands of men to write the Scriptures, only the Holy Spirit Himself fully imparts understanding to us. Man's natural mind is incapable of spiritual insight. Paul said:

"All Scripture is given by inspiration of God, and is profitable for doctrine, for reproof, for correction, for instruction in righteousness, that the man of God may be complete, thoroughly equipped for every good work." (2 Timothy 3:16,17)

I will be bold enough to say that people who do not seek understanding through the power of the Holy Spirit will never fully comprehend the Word of God. They will undoubtedly understand enough Scripture to receive salvation, elementary principles of godly living and an historical foundation in Judeo-Christian ethics. But they will never understand the mysteries of the Spirit recorded in the Word of God.

Revelation comes only through divine impartation

by the Holy Spirit. To receive spiritual understanding in a sermon, both the speaker and the hearer must be under God's anointing. Anointed ears are as important as anointed words in communicating God's will. "Faith comes by hearing . . ." I often tell my congregation to touch their ears and we pray for spiritual anointing on the message as well as the ears of the listeners before I preach.

> *But as it is written: "Eye has not seen, nor ear heard, nor have entered into the heart of man the things which God has prepared for those who love Him." But God has revealed them to us through His Spirit. For the Spirit searches all things, yes, the deep things of God. For what man knows the things of a man except the spirit of the man which is in him? Even so no one knows the things of God except the Spirit of God." (1 Corinthians 2:9-11)*

In our human frame we see only the carnality of man. No man can truly know or judge another with total accuracy. And who of us fully knows about God? Only the Spirit of God is capable of revealing the deep mysteries of God's Word. The unfolding mysteries of God's Word, expounded by human lips, must come through impartation from the Holy Spirit to that vessel called by God as a spokesman. The accountability and responsibility for such a calling is eternal.

We continue reading in Paul's letter to the Corinthians:

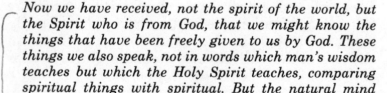

> *Now we have received, not the spirit of the world, but the Spirit who is from God, that we might know the things that have been freely given to us by God. These things we also speak, not in words which man's wisdom teaches but which the Holy Spirit teaches, comparing spiritual things with spiritual. But the natural mind*

*does not receive the things of the Spirit of God, for they
are foolishness to him; nor can he know them, because
they are spiritually discerned. (1 Corinthians 2:12-14)*

No matter how many hours a Bible teacher studies,
without the anointing of the Holy Spirit he will not
teach with authority except in legalistic interpretations of the Word of God. Diligence in Bible study—
though an asset to confidence and intellectual knowledge in teaching the Bible—becomes irrelevant to
opening one to true spiritual enlightenment. A person
may want to know the meaning of Scripture, but he
can't know it fully without the Holy Spirit quicken-
ing his understanding. I do not intend to be judgmen-
tal, but I am convinced that some Bible scholars
holding advanced degrees in theology, even teachers
in seminaries or Bible colleges, have never understood the Word of God by the power of the Holy
Spirit.

Principle number two: **The Word of God was
written to reveal man's final and total victory
in Jesus Christ.** The Bible was not written to promote discussions of such questions as how the sons
of Adam and Eve were able to go to another country
to find wives. Through the years people have argued
about the meaning of such passages in God's Word.
Sometime we miss the major significance of Scripture
messages with diversions on curious details. Then we
debate the details as if they were the central message
of the Bible. The beloved disciple, John, said, "And
truly Jesus did many other signs in the presence of
His disciples, which are not written in this book . . ."
(John 20:30).

Many truths which were not recorded previously
are now being revealed to God's people by the Holy
Spirit. George Frederick Handel, who cloistered him-

self away for three weeks when he wrote "Handel's Messiah," commented that he felt as if he had seen the face of God. Handel's experience is evident in his music. We still sing Handel's *Hallelujah Chorus* today because it expresses such exaltation to God. By the Spirit, we use whatever spiritual enlightenment we receive to magnify God and to minister to His people.

John continued, ". . . but these are written that you may believe that Jesus is the Christ, the Son of God, and that believing you may have life in His name" (John 20:31). Each book of the Bible must be read with the understanding that its central purpose is to bring man to victory through Jesus Christ. Both spiritual warfare and victory always follow enlightenment of God's Word.

Principle number three: **God has a specific message to convey in each book of the Bible.** As we study God's Word, we must search for the core message of each book. For example, Genesis is the book of beginnings. Any new understanding has a point of origin. In Genesis we learn that man was created to be the pleasure of God. We also learn how man "got into trouble." We even catch a glimpse of how he's going to be restored, which is more fully expounded throughout subsequent books of the Bible. All the documented blood relationships recorded throughout the Old Testament are relevant only from a historical perspective, relating to the promise of Jesus Christ as Abraham's Seed. Notice that no lineage of Israel is recorded in Scripture beyond the birth of Jesus.

Some information in the Bible contributes little to the central thrust of Scripture. The major theme of the Bible is recorded in the first few chapters of the Book. Genesis indicates that God ordained, "I put man in a garden to enjoy fellowship with him. He was made in My own likeness. I gave him a choice. He could choose obedience and life, or knowledge of good and evil and death. This choice gave man autonomy. But he fell . . . he blew it! Even then, all was not hopeless. I declared that the offspring of the woman would 'crush the serpent's head' " (Genesis 3:15). Genesis records the first promise of redemption. Promised redemption is the focus of God's message throughout the Old Testament—a promise of restoration to come in the Holy One promised to Israel.

Generations followed man's fall which culminated in Abraham, the first man of faith whom God could trust. I have not forgotten Noah's contribution. God trusted Noah with the preservation of the human race and the animal kingdom, but Noah's life after the flood did not exemplify faith. God trusted Abraham to the extent that He could give him the promise of Jesus Christ, Abraham's Seed (Galatians 3:29).

Although the book of Exodus documents the departure of the children of Israel from Egypt, the main thrust of the book is really the covenant between God and Israel. Even Joseph's reign in Egypt is important only because God kept His covenant with His people who were oppressed. God instructed them to put blood on the doorposts so the death angel would "pass over" their households. The blood of the Lamb became a symbol of covenant extending throughout the entire Bible. The symbols of the plagues recorded in Exodus are the same symbols recorded in the book of Revelation. The Holy Spirit does not change the meaning of symbols He uses, though levels of meaning unfold such as in the parables of Jesus. The Holy Spirit teaches us fresh insights into God's Word and leads us into the application of truth.

Psalms show us how to praise God. The Holy Spirit teaches us to worship God through times of love, pain, despair, joy and trust which are recorded in the Psalms. When the Spirit brings the Psalms alive, worship is lifted to the same dimension of God's presence that David experienced. Whenever people worship scripturally by the letter of the law, they strive to maintain forms, rituals, and precise wording. They go through the motions, but never really enter into intimate communion with God.

The purpose of the gospels is to bring "good news." Matthew announces good news from the standpoint of the King and the Kingdom. Mark's good news stresses the tremendous urgency of the message. Luke, the gentle physician, emphasizes the compassion of Christ as Healer and Teacher. John was the writer called as a "revelator." John portrays Christ with an intimacy of knowing His heart as nobody else did. All biblical discussions beyond the "good news" of Jesus Christ's Kingdom can become argumentative and sometimes even jell into divisive doctrines. Christ came to seek and to save "that which was lost." God so loved the world that He sent Jesus to redeem creation from bondage. Jesus is coming back to earth to establish His Kingdom forever. Now, that's good news!

The Acts of the Apostles demonstrate that the Holy Spirit is the source of the witness and power of the Church. The epistles are written messages of instruction, giving applications of the gospel of Jesus Christ. The epistles were written by apostles to individual churches. If a church does not have the same problems as the church at Corinth, we shouldn't worry about every detail that Paul wrote to that church. Sometimes we try to read instructions into these letters that God is not giving to us today at all. But whenever we encounter similar circumstances or problems, the Holy Spirit says, "Here is the way to handle this situation."

The last book of the Bible, The Revelation of Jesus Christ, is a series of visions given to John on the Isle of Patmos. This book shows man's final and total victory over Satan and the restoration of all things. John records his visions of Jesus from various perspectives: Christ, the Candlestick among the churches; Christ, the slain Lamb of God; Christ, the coming King and Ruler.

God has something special to say in each book of the Bible. When the books are compiled as a single consensus of "God speaking to man," they proclaim the message mankind needs to accomplish God's purposes on the earth.

Principle number four: **Determine by the Holy Spirit to whom God is communicating.** The gospels apparently communicate to the whole world: "For God so loved the world . . ." (John 3:16). The Holy Spirit addresses Jewish Christians in the book of Hebrews. He says, "You had one covenant, but God has provided a better covenant." The entire book of Hebrews emphasizes the new covenant relationship to Jewish Christians.

Paul's Corinthian letters illustrate numerous principles of church structure. According to historical records, approximately thirty to forty thousand Christians lived at Corinth when Paul wrote to them. Although they did not all assemble at the same place, they were members of only one church, not several individuals churches. The Corinthian Christians had many shepherds. When the Apostle Paul came to Corinth, he served as their final authority in spiritual decisions.

The Christians held fellowship meetings with their shepherds at various sites around Corinth. On the occasions when the whole church worshiped together, people gathered from all parts of the city. Some rode to church in their big chariots, bringing fine wines and sumptuous food. They assembled in their own elite groups to eat, drink and fellowship. Others from poorer communities sometimes didn't have enough food to feed their families. Those with an abundance of food and wine gorged themselves, and even became drunk, while other people went hungry. When Paul observed what was happening, he reprimanded the people. "What? Have you not houses to eat and to drink in? Or despise you the Church of God, and shame them that have not?"

In most churches today, I'm happy to say that drunken revelry is not a problem as it was at Corinth. We have no reason to spiritualize Paul's admonishment on this subject when the circumstances don't apply. Perhaps the principle for us is sharing with impoverished brothers and sisters in Christ out of our abundance. We must know to whom and in what circumstances God is speaking in Scripture to make adequate application to our own lives in twentieth century circumstances.

Paul wrote letters to Timothy as a spiritual father addresses his beloved son. Although some of the advice he gave Timothy may not be important to us today, many principles of leadership in ministry which Paul shared with Timothy are pertinent. The subject matter also guides any elder or older spiritual leader in instructing a younger spiritual person (younger in spiritual experience, not in age). Paul rightly said to Timothy as well as to the early

Church, "You have many teachers in the faith, but few fathers" (1 Corinthians 4:15-17).

The Holy Spirit speaks in Revelation to persecuted Christians, giving them hope and comfort. The symbolic language in the book is utilized to give a powerful message, yet to protect readers from further persecution if the manuscript is seized by adverse government authorities. For that reason, a modern reader must have knowledge of Old Testament symbolism to understand the message of Revelation. When the Spirit described a "beast with seven heads," the Roman emperor did not recognize that description to mean anything more than a literal, multi-headed beast. But to Jewish Christians, their Scriptures taught that "a beast" represented earthly authority. They knew that a seven-headed beast represented a government in total authority. The number seven always symbolized perfection to the Jews.

John, who was exiled on the Isle of Patmos as a form of persecution, recorded his vision as exhortation and encouragement to other persecuted Christians around the world. He used symbols under the direction of the Holy Spirit. If he had not written in symbols, his message would likely have been destroyed. The officials who censored John's manuscript read, "Beasts ... Frogs ... An animal with power in its tail ..." They thought, "That's ridiculous! It doesn't mean anything! Give it to them."

However, persecuted Christians knew exactly what John intended them to know. His symbolism derived directly from their cultural heritage. So the book of Revelation was written to Christian people, showing them God's plan from the incarnation of Christ to the mission of the Church today. I believe the Church now stands near the end of John's Revelation.

Principle number five: **Acknowledge the frame of reference of both the writer and the reading audience.** First of all, note the location of people to whom the message is addressed. A message sent to Rome will have a totally different flavor than one sent to Ephesus. Then note the circumstances at the writing of the message. John's Revelation is read by Christians who faced severe persecution. Some letters were addressed to affluent people in certain churches. The church at Corinth faced unusual cultural influences, such as not being able to distinguish the men from the women. Paul asked them, "Doesn't nature teach you certain things? The looks of a woman should be distinguishable from the looks of a man" (1 Corinthians 11:13-16). This advice was specifically addressed to the circumstances at that church. Through legalistic interpretations, some churches have built entire doctrines based on dress codes for women. How sad!

What are the symbols the writer uses and why does he use them? The numbers "seven" and "ten" always mean perfection. The word "mountain" often symbolizes a kingdom. When John spoke about "a mountain" in Revelation, Jewish Christians understood his inference immediately. I suspect that the Jews knew Jesus spoke metaphorically when He said, "Speak to this mountain (kingdom), and it shall be removed." Seemingly difficult passages become simple concepts of faith when we allow the Holy Spirit to give us understanding.

Principle number six: **Never interpret the Scriptures to prove a doctrine, principle or method, but only to find the purpose or goal of that scriptural passage.** Jesus clearly warned, "You teach for doctrine the traditions of men" (Matthew 15:9). Some denominations have been built around religious traditions. For example, differences in the meaning and methods of water baptism have caused much division in the Church. Modes and methods of baptism were not important to the early Church, or the Scriptures would have been more specific in describing a procedure for administering the sacrament. God was emphasizing, "I'm going to make a covenant with man. Baptism begins your discipleship training." If a person were in a desert without water, God would not require him to be immersed in water.

Strict adherence to the letter of the law kills, but the Holy Spirit makes the Word of God come alive. Sadly, today most interpretations of scriptures derive from meanings based on the letter of the law and not by the Holy Spirit. Many churches are dying for that reason.

Principle number seven: **Remain open to fresh insights and understanding of Scripture.** Previous insights, if they are from God, point us in a direction which will never vary. Fresh understanding makes the basic foundations of Scripture we previously accepted more solid within us as God uncovers further insights into His plan. In these last days, the Holy Spirit is opening understanding to God's people which we could not comprehend previously. Paul said, "But we speak the wisdom of God in a mystery, the hidden wisdom which God ordained before the ages for our glory . . ." (1 Corinthians 2:7).

Suppose a child entering the first grade heard the teacher say, "Today we're going to study trigonometry." Those students' comprehension of advanced mathematics would be impossible. No, a teacher begins by saying, "If you had one apple and I had one apple, and we put these apples together, how many apples would we have?" God reveals to us only knowledge which He can trust us to implement. He shares with us whatever we need to know for our needs or the needs of our generation. If God reveals truth for another time, He specifies to whom the revelation is intended.

For instance, God gave revelation to Daniel which he couldn't understand. When Daniel questioned God concerning the revelation, God said, "Go your way, Daniel, for the words are closed up and sealed till the time of the end" (Daniel 12:9). Many of the seals on revelation recorded in Scripture are open to the generation who will welcome Jesus Christ, the King, at His return.

Paul received such high levels of revelation that God had to show him how to maintain equilibrium with his natural mind. Some people place such an emphasis on spiritual insights that they become "no earthly good" to others. God can only trust us with knowledge to the level of our ability to respond in the Spirit and live out the understanding He gives to us. Why would God give us principles requiring greater spiritual maturity when we are still jealous or competitive with other Christians? The writer of Hebrews understood this truth when he wrote, "I want to give you spiritual meat, but I have to take you back to the very first principles of faith over and over again. I'd like to move beyond spiritual milk, but you don't seem to understand basic teaching. I can't give you revelation intended for mature believers" (Hebrews 5:12-14).

If God trusts the Church with demonstrating the vision He's put into my heart, He is calling for mature, discerning Christians for whom He can show Himself strong in their behalf. If we don't respond, God will remove opportunities from us. He will reserve the opportunity to be His final witness for another generation. Our responsiveness to God's Word is absolutely essential. A principle of the Kingdom is, "I'll trust you with a few tasks. If you show yourself to be responsible, I will give you more authority." Our thinking usually bargains, "God, give me responsibility and honor. I'll prove to You that I can be faithful." Never! God says, "Be faithful in small things. Then I'll give you greater responsibilities." God never, absolutely never breaks that principle!

Jesus taught the parable of the talents in which one man received five talents and another received only one. A "talent" represents the potential within a person. Most of us could easily identify one talent within us, but instead of utilizing one talent with faithfulness, often we complain. We feel jealous of the one who receives two or five talents. If we fail to use God's gifts, He eventually removes even that one talent from us. That's the Kingdom principle.

Paul received revelations which allowed him to comprehend truth that others would consider to be unlawful (2 Corinthians 12:4). He was careful not to offend people by his high level of revelation from God since he was called to be their servant and bring them to maturity. The Holy Spirit gives understanding to mature Christians which others can't receive. Spiritual maturity demands a solid scriptural foundation of truth and actions which prove trustworthiness before God. Immature Christians abuse revelation. They misunderstand spiritual freedom of God's grace. Without revelation of the Holy Spirit, such "freedom" always results in unrighteousness or arrogance. Paul said, "Because I live in this level of spiritual comprehension, I will be very careful not to offend you by the insights that God has given me" (Romans 14:12-19).

Because we live in the last days, just before the coming of Christ, Satan will spare nothing to deceive the very elect. Opportunities open to us require greater responsibility, demonstration of righteousness and comprehension of God's Word than ever before. Persecution toward anointed ministries demands a commitment of unity among God's covenant people. God trusts us with truth which will enable us to endure and prevail in any test.

Still, Satan comes against us with powerful tactics. He intends to steal our understanding and cause divisions among us. Pressures now focus primarily on Kingdom demonstration in families, covenant relationships in the Church, and business decisions that test our obedience to God. The Bible says that the Kingdom message will bring a sword to divide those who "will" from those who "will not" follow the Lord (Matthew 10:34). We must be able to discern what is God's direction and what "opportunities" only divert our attention away from God's perfect will for our lives.

The Holy Spirit gives fresh insights into God's Word to motivate us for fulfilling His purposes. God allows us to experience trials to test our faith and determine whether we are sensitive to His Spirit's direction. For that reason, God's enlightenment grants an increased measure of authority to the Church in these last days. He knows we need His authority to combat the wiles of Satan and to demonstrate the adequate witness as a standard of righteousness. Only then can Christ judge the world according to the standard of His witness in the earth.

6

THEOLOGICAL PRESUPPOSITIONS

Many critics of ministries today claim that they speak as "Bereans." They insist that their critiques are submitted to the body of Christ as those merely validating preachers' messages as being biblically sound. Paul, Silas and Timothy visited Berea, a populous city of southwest Macedonia, on their second missionary journey. The Book of Acts records that the Bereans, ". . . received the word with all readiness, and searched the Scriptures daily to find out whether those things were so. Therefore many of them believed . . ." (Acts 17:11,12).

Paul leaves Berea hurriedly. Hostile Jews from Thessalonica followed the apostles to Berea and began refuting Paul's message (Acts 17:13,14). I believe that some of the critics calling themselves "Bereans" are more easily compared to the Jews from Thessalonica. They target their warnings toward those who "received the word with all readiness, and searched the Scriptures." The results sometimes destroy seeds of life which are sown.

What was Paul's message to the Bereans that generated such joy in some people and hostility in others? From Paul's epistles we know he simply proclaimed: Jesus Christ is "God in the flesh, the living Word of God. Jesus fulfilled the Law and the Prophets' promises of redemption as the Messiah sent from God. Through salvation in Him, all have access to His life of love and power by the indwelling Holy Spirit within us. We are His body in the world today, the on-going incarnation of God, revealing Jesus Christ's good news of hope and restoration to a lost and dying world."

The majority of Christians give intellectual assent to that New Testament message. But people who simply know truth do not significantly threaten the kingdom of darkness. Thousands of born-again Christians say and think the truths of God's Word. Sadly, too few Christians actually experience the fires of boldness which "turn the world upside down" as members of the early Church did (Acts 17:6). Satan wars implementation of God's Word with all the power at his command. Scriptural enlightenment ignites fires of witness within Christians. God's Word bursts into life within believers who live and move on the basis of covenant with God. They fight oppressive forces with spiritual weapons to the extent that they "love not their lives unto death." These Christians cause the kingdoms of this world to totter in

[handwritten marginal note: ✓ but those who live out.]

fear.

When we examine the arguments of these so-called "Bereans" closely, we recognize that their contentions are usually based on the mind of reason. Their arguments attempt to relegate miracles of the Spirit through the Church to the confinement of the first century. A major premise on which they build their case claims that "God is not bound by His law." They accuse those believing in miracles of God for today as trying to "make Christianity scientific." This attack is specifically aimed at "word of faith" teachers—Kenneth Hagin, Ken Copeland, Charles Capps, and others—who are portrayed as holding God to "cause and effect" guarantees in Scripture. "Prosperity" promises in Scripture are also under fire. The critics claim that "prosperity" concepts related to "faith" allow people to believe that they can force God to act according to their will. "Faith" (as taught in ministries under attack) is portrayed as man's manipulating God's Word to get whatever he wants.

This attack on Christians who move in the supernatural realm of miracles of God is built on the critic's theological presupposition that "God is not bound by law." I strongly disagree with that premise. The essence of "miracles" is that they break laws established and honored by God at creation! Laws in both the natural and the supernatural realm must exist if God's intervention to accomplish His purposes allows for a miracle to occur. For instance, Enoch's translation from "life to eternal life" without experiencing physical death defied the law for mortality of man's flesh. We are not told the means by which Enoch was "translated," but the experience surely violated the natural laws of gravity at the very

101

least (Genesis 5:24). Certainly a "floating ax head" violated the law of gravity (2 Kings 6:6).

Miracles move beyond natural law which God established in creation of the physical world. I want to emphasize that God established laws governing creation and life both in the natural and spiritual realms. God limits Himself to work within the laws He ordains. Though God is sovereign, He keeps His Word. Man's obedience and faith toward God allow miracles—supernatural occurrences overriding natural laws—to occur. Why? Miracles alert mankind to the knowledge of God's omnipotence and the implementation of His eternal plan. Miracles follow faith and obedience to God's Word as confirmation of His truth. We know from Scripture that God desires to interact with His creation. The epitome of God's interaction with man was demonstrated in the ministry of Jesus.

Critics claim that since miracles, by their definition, are not governed by laws of any kind, no formal prayers or demands upon God can bring about a miracle. I answer that claim by agreeing that miracles are not governed by any ritualistic formulas or prayers. No "magic words" make something happen by the Spirit of God. However, miracles do operate by the law of obedience and faith in God's Word. God honors His Word and His will. Many of His own promises to covenant people defy natural laws and certainly are contrary to the mind of reason.

The valid danger of some "faith teaching," which gives ammunition to the critics' arguments, is that too often Christians receive scriptural promises as "blanket statements." Spiritual laws and natural laws do not operate in the same indiscriminate way. Instead of believing for a miracle in specific situations according to the leading of the Holy Spirit, often Christians regard God's Word as unreliable. They are disappointed in their answers to prayer. Their circumstances do not meet their own criteria for desired results. Yet faith and obedience are basic ingredients of establishing one's relationship with God. Applications of a "formula" for a good relationship are always contingent upon the personalities, maturity and commitment within that relationship.

In applying laws of faith the primary criteria for "asking in My name" is the will and purposes of God. God's miraculous power always benefits the purposes of His Kingdom first. Secondly, they benefit the purposes of God in the life of the one who is asking in faith. God consistently grants the petitions of those who are "one in Spirit," or abiding with Him. Jesus said, "If you abide in Me, and My words abide in you, you will ask what you desire, and it shall be done for you" (John 15:7).

Miracles always have purpose in accord with God's will and plan. Many miracles in the Old Testament preserved the nation of Israel from annihilation. Miracles of the apostles confirmed their message and brought curious crowds to hear the gospel of Jesus Christ. Jesus performed miracles in fulfillment of messianic prophecy—sending word to John the Baptist by his disciples that His works confirmed that He was the promised One from God. But to suggest that miracles negate God's honoring His natural and spiritual laws leads one to question the authority of God's Word rather than confirming the fulfillment of it.

God cannot lie (Titus 1:2). The basis of truth is law, order, design and absolute standards by which we measure "right" and "wrong." God by His own power and omnipotence set standards in His Word which

He honors irrefutably. God speaks laws into existence. To change God's laws means that God changes His own nature, which is impossible. Assumptions that God does not honor His law leave people responding to a God who seems to be moody, acting according to His whims on a certain day. This view is hardly the nature of God personified in Jesus Christ's ministry. The writer of Hebrews said:

> *Thus God, determining to show more abundantly to the heirs of promise the immutability of His counsel, confirmed it by an oath, **that by two immutable things, in which it is impossible for God to lie,** we might have strong consolation, who have fled for refuge to lay hold of the hope set before us. This hope we have as an anchor of the soul, both sure and steadfast, and which enters the Presence behind the veil, where the forerunner has entered for us, even Jesus, having become High Priest forever according to the order of Melchizedek. (Hebrews 6:17-20)*

Once God makes a promise, He will not break His Word. Miracles become a trajectory of His character, only interrupting natural laws for the benefit of His sovereign plan. Miracles lift natural laws to spiritual dimensions in human experience. Peter said that everything is held by the Word of God.

> *But the heavens and the earth which now exist are kept in store **by the same word,** reserved for fire until the day of judgment and perdition of ungodly men." (2 Peter 3:7)*

God's immutable laws assure us that even though Satan's forces attack righteousness in our world, chaos and rebellion will eventually be conquered. At Christ's coming, God's order and design will reign throughout eternity. Let's examine some immutable laws which God has given to His covenant people:

"Again I say to you that if two of you agree on earth concerning anything that they ask, it will be done for them by My Father in heaven." (Matthew 18:19)

Beloved, if our heart does not condemn us, we have confidence toward God. And whatever we ask we receive from Him, because we keep His commandments and do those things that are pleasing in His sight. (1 John 3:21,22)

Do not be deceived, God is not mocked; for whatever a man sows, that will he also reap. For he who sows to his flesh will of the flesh reap corruption, but he who sows to the Spirit will of the Spirit reap everlasting life. (Galatians 6:7,8)

"Give, and it will be given to you . . ." (Luke 6:38)

". . . if My people who are called by My name will humble themselves, and pray and seek My face, and turn from their wicked ways, then I will hear from heaven, and will forgive their sin and heal their land." (2 Chronicles 7:14)

These scriptures only begin the list of spiritual "laws" which God honors in dealing with His covenant people. An obvious question is whether God's laws work for unbelievers. The answer is yes and no. Some laws governing natural relationships work for both believers and non-believers. God's promise of "long life" to those "honoring father and mother" could encompass non-believers growing up in non-Christian families (Exodus 20:12).

Scriptures governing personal attitudes such as, "A soft answer turns away wrath" (Proverbs 15:1), or "A man who has friends must himself be friendly . . ." (Proverbs 18:24) work for anyone—Christian or non-Christian—applying those principles. Secular seminars on "Winning Friends and Influencing Others" are based on simple laws of Scripture which apply in all human interaction. Such seminars seldom give the source of such powerful insights, but they work for the one practicing them regardless of His beliefs about God.

I've already discussed the power of unity to accomplish good or evil purposes as demonstrated at the Tower of Babel. God confused the people's language because using His law of unity, ". . . nothing that they propose to do will be withheld from them" (Genesis 11:6). Supernatural intervention from God was necessary. God recognized that He was bound by His own law—first, the power of unity; secondly, dealing with man's wickedness. God's primary purposes for His creation were threatened. God interrupted the law of unity at a dimension requiring even division among mankind (by languages) to counter man's evil plan.

The opposite of God's intervention at the Tower of Babel occurred at Pentecost. The people gathered in a room in one mind and in one accord. By the power of the Holy Spirit falling upon them, they spoke in languages they had never learned. The Bible said that people in Jerusalem heard the gospel in their own language. Believers rushed out into the streets as empowered witnesses to the gospel of Jesus Christ as a result of coming into unity of Spirit in the upper room (Acts 2:1-8).

Most of God's promises will not work for unbelievers. His benefits demand covenant between man and Himself. Jesus told His disciples that certain demonic spirits were cast out ". . . by nothing but prayer and fasting" (Mark 9:29). An unbeliever attempting to use that law would commit blasphemy. An unbeliever would be using evil to cast out evil—dividing the kingdom of darkness. People in deception lose the standard of God's laws by attempting to manipulate them for their own purposes. God's standard is His Kingdom—righteousness, peace and joy in the Holy Spirit. Anyone attempting to use God's laws with motives contrary to "righteousness, peace and joy in the Holy Spirit" moves in deception.

Unbelievers can never receive the promises of God extended only to covenant people. ". . . all things work together for good . . ." only applies ". . . to those who love God, to those who are the called according to His purpose" (Romans 8:28). ". . . fellowship with one another, and the blood of Jesus Christ His Son cleanses us from all sin" applies only to those who "walk in the light as He is in the light" (1 John 1:7). One promise of healing the sick is contingent upon recognizing eldership within the body of Christ who pray the "prayer of faith" (James 5:14,15).

God's laws can be misused. Deceived people will come to Jesus asking, ". . . have we not . . . cast out demons in Your name . . .?" (Matthew 7:22). The sons of Sceva attempted to cast out devils by "the Jesus whom Paul preaches" and were physically attacked by the demonic forces (Acts 19:13-16). Sometimes worldly people build prosperous businesses by using Kingdom principles of excellence and servanthood. Their improper motives eventually cause their humanistic empires to crumble. "I have seen the wicked in great power, and spreading himself like a native green tree, yet he passed away, and behold, he was no more . . ." (Psalm 37:35,36). People build hospitals, orphanages, and charitable organizations to aid the infirmed, believing that their benevolence will justify them before God in eternity. The world honors such philanthropists for their good deeds, but God does not. Works of the flesh, no matter how noble, are humanistic and will perish.

I believe the theological presupposition that "God is not bound by His own law" is the most dangerous argument that Dave Hunt proposes in *Seduction of Christianity*, but it is certainly not the only one. I am concerned at the definitions of key words on which Mr. Hunt builds his arguments. For instance, the word "sorcery" is applied to the teaching of some of the most fruitful contemporary ministries in the world—ministries through which millions of people have come to know Jesus Christ. The implications of such accusations become a serious affront to the work of evangelism around the world.

To accuse leaders of God's people of deliberately using witchcraft or evil powers to mislead those seeking spiritual answers is the most serious charge that could be made against them. Exposing faults of personal character would be far less significant. Accusing a minister of practicing "sorcery" should never be confused with godly admonition or correction for error in doctrine. Even then, correction must come from proven eldership in the body of Christ. These statements are not spoken in "brotherly love," nor are they intended to bring healing or unity to the body of Christ. I don't even believe they are spoken necessarily with the intention of bringing division among Christians, though they do.

Regardless of the critics' motives, Satan is the accuser of the brethren and his motives are clear. He attacks the most productive members of the body of Christ, intending to kill or hinder their witness. Robert Schuller, accused of "sorcery" in Dave Hunt's *Seduction of Christianity*, is perhaps reaching more non-Christians through television and books than any other religious leader in America (Hunt, p.15). Another accused "seducer," Paul Yonggi Cho, is senior pastor of the largest church in the world—one-half million members—in Seoul, Korea (Hunt, pp.16, 25,33,113). Consider the reasons these particular pastors were chosen by the author as example "sorcerers." Their notoriety insures that his book is marketable. The validity of their ministries is called into question by many people who stand on the periphery of following their teaching. Controversy sells. Mixing enough commonly known teaching from some people associated with the occult, along with innuendos and quotes from well-known Christian leaders creates irresistible intrigue.

The messages of these ministries are cited as being part of the "last days' deception" prophesied in Scripture. Assumptions concerning "The Antichrist" are discussed throughout the book as if all Christians agree on the character, nature and historical role of this person (Hunt, pp.37,49). Scriptures taken from the Revelation of Jesus Christ are used as if all Christians agreed on one single dispensational interpretation (Hunt, pp.47-51). Seldom do these writers use the reference to the "spirit of antichrist" about which John said, ". . . which you have heard was coming, and is now already in the world" (1 John 4:3).

The "rapture," a word not used in Scripture but widely taught in evangelical circles, becomes an accepted presupposition for the future departure of the Church (Hunt, p.64). Many Christians anticipate a "catching away" of the Church that supposedly could occur at any moment. Yet Jesus said that the end would be "as the days of Noah were" in which the wicked were "taken" while Noah and his family remained on the earth (Matthew 24:37-39). The parable of the "wheat and tares" indicates that in the "time of harvest" the "tares" were uprooted and destroyed while the "wheat" was gathered into the barn (Matthew 13:30). And almost no one anticipating the "rapture" taking them into the sky looks forward to Jesus' promise that "the meek shall inherit the earth" (Matthew 5:5).

Dave Hunt refers to the founding of national Israel as significant in determining the season of the end times (Hunt, p.38). The role of modern Israel in prophecy varies among Christians who believe that "circumcision of heart" designates one to be "Abraham's seed" (Romans 2:29). Mr. Hunt makes references to "the temple" to be built in Jerusalem before Christ's return (Hunt, p.54). Again, the construction of a literal "temple" is a presupposition. Many Christians view the end time "temple" as God's holy people—a temple "not made with hands" like the stone recorded in the Book of Daniel which eventually encompassed the whole earth (Daniel 2:35). Certainly the "temple" referred to in John's Revelation is clearly "not made with hands."

> *And I heard a loud voice from heaven saying, "Behold, the tabernacle of God is with men, and He will dwell with them, and they shall be His people, and God Himself will be with them and be their God." (Revelation 21:3)*

And verse 22 states:

> *But I saw no temple in it, for the Lord God Almighty and the Lamb are its temple.*

One major theological problem for Christians who believe in the literal reconstruction of a temple is the practice of animal sacrifices. The New Testament book of Hebrews clearly indicates that the blood of Christ ended the sacrifices of bulls and goats for sins as practiced by the Jews.

Now where there is remission of these, there is no longer an offering for sin. Therefore, brethren, having boldness to enter the Holiest by the blood of Jesus, by a new and living way He consecrated for us, through the veil, that is, His flesh . . . (Hebrews 10:18-20)

Other presuppositions have to do with heaven and the Marriage Supper of the Lamb. People who teach "prosperity" are accused of being uninterested in going to heaven and feasting at the Marriage Supper of the Lamb at the rapture (Hunt, p.66). What do such suppositions do in interpreting Jesus' announcement that "the Kingdom of heaven is **at hand**" (Matthew 3:2; 4:17; 10:7)? What arguments equate poverty and lack of material resources with "heavenly minded-ness"? If poverty created mature Christians, the most spiritually mature people in the world would live in the most impoverished countries. Such statements use biblical assumptions to justify serious charges against ministries. Christian writers have a right to state their views and interpretations of Scripture, but to call ministers "sorcerers" based on presupposed theological views is highly irresponsible.

Good intentions often lead people down a road of deception. We must examine motives carefully to discern truth. The fruit of ministries becomes obvious upon close examination. Responsible Christians need to heed the biblical warning to "know those who labor among you" (1 Thessalonians 5:12).

We should not accept someone's opinions at face value. Examine an author's ministry as well as the ministries of those he names. Are people restored? Are they loving Jesus more and seeking His Kingdom in their daily lives? Are they understanding covenant with God and discipleship? We discern the counterfeit by knowing the real. A man who has received a vision from God will never be convinced by anyone that he has been deceived. A woman who has received a miracle from God will never allow someone to tell her that miracles ended with the first century apostles. The Apostle Paul built his entire ministry on the vision of Jesus calling him into the ministry. He said, ". . . I was not disobedient to the heavenly vision . . ." (Acts 26:19). How do Christians avoid deception?

First, to avoid deception, a person must have a personal relationship with Jesus Christ. Jesus said, "My sheep hear My voice, and I know them, and they follow Me" (John 10:27). Knowing Jesus helps us to discern contrary winds of doctrine which grieve the Holy Spirit within us. We also can easily receive correction and admonition which comes from God. When a Christian is chastened by the Lord, he feels genuine conviction. Instead of feeling accused, he feels a longing for the sense of peace and joy which come from a right relationship with the Lord.

I was the first Pentecostal-born young man to graduate from a seminary. I attended a Methodist seminary, Candler School of Theology at Emory University in Atlanta. I remember some interesting discussions in my seminary classes about the "Pentecostal experience" of speaking in tongues. Some of my professors were hard-nosed skeptics toward certain ministry gifts of the Holy Spirit. I can remember specific discussions on whether the "experience" was demonic. Those discussions never shook my faith whatsoever. I knew!

As a young man of twelve, I had watched a dying

woman praying in a spiritual language. I knew that this woman's words were spoken to God. Later that year, my own experience of receiving the baptism of the Holy Spirit left me with a confidence in the Lord that was unshakable. I had grown up as the son of a Pentecostal preacher. As a precocious young man, I had seen enough "counterfeits" in church to question the validity of the experience. But God has a way of answering genuine questions of the heart. I "knew that I knew" the real experience, and no intellectual, academic discussions could ever rob that experience from me.

Secondly, we avoid deception when we know the character of God. God is the same yesterday, today and forever (Hebrews 13:8). God's character always depicts love. To love is to give oneself in the interest of others. Love is the strength of our covenant with God because we can trust Him to direct our paths. His love endures any tests. God's character is truth. The mark of spirituality is loving truth and pleasing God. God is righteous, but He is also full of mercy and grace. His law convicts us of sin, His love brings us to Him, and His mercy deals with our transgressions. The goodness of God works repentance in our hearts.

Thirdly, we avoid deception by knowing the Word of God. Deception comes to those who manipulate God's Word to prove their case rather than accepting the spirit of His Word as it is written. Genuine prophesy is not to be interpreted, but received and judged for whatever it says. God always confirms His prophetic Word. We must hear and understand God's Word, "hiding His Word in our hearts" to keep us from sin and deception (Psalm 119:11). Jesus answered Satan's temptations by replying, "It is written . . ." We must follow His example when temptations come.

God's Word is spoken by holy men today just as when the Bible was written. Some people point to the passage in Revelation which says, "I testify to everyone who hears the words of the prophecy of this book: If anyone adds to these things, God will add to him the plagues that are written in this book; and if anyone takes away from the words of the book of this prophecy, God shall take away his part from the Book of Life, from the holy city, and from the things which are written in this book" (Revelation 22:18,19). These verses mean exactly what they say. Anyone adding to or taking away from The Revelation of Jesus Christ is accursed. Jesus is a complete revelation of God to man and of man to God. No one adds or subtracts from the revelation of His identity, or John's Revelation of Him! Also, remember that such a curse may have preserved the manuscript under the conditions in which John wrote it.

Fourthly, we avoid deception when we learn how to honor spiritual authority. Paul wrote, "O foolish Galatians!" I brought you to truth, "Who has bewitched you . . . ?" (Galatians 3:1). We must learn the source of true spiritual authority. True authority is never abusive or striving. True spiritual leaders gently lead their sheep. God's leaders exemplify the qualities of good parents—instilling values which bring people to maturity in the Lord. Paul wrote, "And we urge you, brethren, to recognize those who labor among you, and are over you in the Lord and admonish you, and to esteem them very highly in love for their work's sake. Be at peace among yourselves" (1 Thessalonians 5:12,13).

Finally, we avoid deception when we stay

open to correction. Even the most spiritually mature Christians have blind spots and weak areas in which they must be "fitly joined together" for the work of the ministry. The attribute of humility is staying open for correction before God. God honors a "contrite heart" that is willing to admit mistakes. God's Word teaches that in a "multitude of counselors, there is safety" (Proverbs 11:14). Submission to eldership for correction is one of the most mature attitudes a Christian can have. Again, unity of the body of Christ is necessary to accomplish His will in the earth. No one has all the answers. God gives various ministries pieces of the puzzle which fit with other pieces to bring us to the image of Christ (Ephesians 4:13). God has specifically charged me with the message of "Kingdom" teaching. Another brings the message of the "Word of faith" or "Healing" or "Intercession" to the body of Christ. All are necessary components of the full counsel of God in demonstrating His Word in our generation.

Together we are "iron sharpening iron" (Proverbs 27:17) and "deep calling unto deep" (Psalm 42:7). When the body of Christ is moving as one body, we will not be tossed to and fro by winds of doctrine. We will hear clearly the wind of the Holy Spirit and move only at His command. Our goal must be to come into full maturity and love. Then the Spirit and the bride say together, "Come, Lord Jesus, Come . . ."

7

TRUE SEDUCTION OF CHRISTIANITY

Spiritual deception reminds me of a children's story that everyone has heard, "Little Red Riding Hood." This story depicts deception as the proverbial "wolf in sheep's clothing" [or, in this case, Grandma's]. Such false identity is the case with deception in the Church today. At times it seems that voices warning of deception become the seducers themselves. They quote Scripture, write Christian books, speak on Christian radio and television programs, and their warnings confuse many Christians seeking truth in God's Word. They target warnings of error toward some of the most anointed, fruitful ministries in the Church today.

Jesus confronted those who opposed His mission from God with the words:

"Woe to you! For you build the tombs of the prophets, and your fathers killed them. In fact, you bear witness that you approve the deeds of your fathers; for they indeed killed them, and you build their tombs. Therefore the wisdom of God also said, 'I will send them prophets and apostles, and some of them they will kill and persecute,' that the blood of all the prophets which was shed from the foundation of the world may be required of this generation, from the blood of Abel to the blood of Zechariah who perished between the altar and the temple. Yes, I say to you, it shall be required of this generation. Woe to you lawyers! For you have taken away the key of knowledge. You did not enter in yourselves, and those who were entering in you hindered." (Luke 11:47-52)

As in Jesus' day, we live in a world where certain spiritual teachers and lawyers (legalistic theologians), either knowingly through satanic deception or deliberately, attempt to "kill the prophets" who speak God's Word to our generation. Those who can't refute the message of prophets resort to attacking God's messengers themselves. They attempt to discredit ministers and ministries. Messengers who bring unfolding insights into God's Word are linked with those recognized as being mystical in their teaching. Christian teachers—Paul Yonggi Cho, Agnes Sanford, Robert Schuller, Robert Tilton and others—are accused of promoting sorcery, Eastern religions and apostate doctrines.

The critics, justifying concerns at such dangerous teaching as that espoused by groups like the New Age, only add fuel to the arguments of people refuting a genuine move of God today. Certain writers capitalize on Christians' fears of apostate doctrines. They ignore the spiritual fruit of ministries as a valid confirmation of God's blessing. Many critics who are dispensationalists, such as Dave Hunt, do not believe in the operation of supernatural gifts of the Holy Spirit in our day. They claim to be "literalists," yet they are offended at teachers who exhort Christians to receive and exercise spiritual gifts in ministry as taught in God's Word (1 Corinthians 12 and 14; John 16:13).

The lack of biblical foundation for charges made against Christian ministers today is appalling. Accusations are based on occult research. The final authorities for derogatory claims become the writers themselves. Their critiques, perhaps unintentionally, attempt to "kill" prophetic voices.

Associating similarities in the messages of Christian ministers to non-Christians and occult leaders plant confusion and doubt in readers' minds. A critic's failure to follow scriptural instructions in confronting those whom he considers to be teaching apostate doctrines calls his true intentions into question. The offense of a brother is obviously less important than the urgency of public reprimand. Christians need to ask themselves the reasons for such urgency.

Written controversy and accusations sell, but at such a price to God's people! Inevitably, the fruit of controversy causes "little ones" to stumble. Nonbelievers simply close their ears to the Church's message of redemption at hearing our internal bickering. People seeking the truth of God's Word withdraw from ministers genuinely called by God in His fivefold ministry. The Holy Spirit is grieved. The Church divides, paying a high price with grave, eternal consequences.

Let's examine a *Webster's Dictionary* definition of

"seduction" to identify the real seducers of Christianity. "**Seduction**: 1. to purposely mislead someone; 2. an effort to persuade one into disloyalty." Allow me to add to the dictionary definition with further denotation of the word "seduction" applied as spiritual definitions which I believe that God has shown me. "**Seduction**: 1. consciously taking control of another by lustful, lewd practices or thoughts; an appeal to one's appetites to purposely teach error; 2. to prostitute, dilute or compromise the message of truth given by God through His recorded Word."

Points To Define Spiritual Seduction

I wish to further define "seduction" with eighteen points which I believe expose deception in the Church. Let me emphasize that I wish to expose deception, not "flesh and blood." Satan is the "deceiver," and we must seek the Lord to unmask the source of Satan's influence so that we can loose and bind spiritual opposition to God's will according to His Word.

1. **Failing to be led by true, revealed authority by purposely limiting true knowledge of God.** "The secret things belong to the Lord our God, but those things which are **revealed** belong to us and to our children forever, that we may do all the words of this law" (Deuteronomy 29:29). "Surely the Lord God does nothing, unless **He reveals** His secret to His servants the prophets" (Amos 3:7).

2. **Substituting the mind of reason (human intellect) for obedience to God.** A major example of this "seduction" is the reasoning of the serpent speaking to Eve in the Garden of Eden. Paul wrote, "But I fear, lest somehow, as the serpent deceived Eve by his craftiness, so your minds may be cor-

rupted from the simplicity that is in Christ" (2 Corinthians 11:3).

3. **Pursuing truth to serve one's own appetites or ambitions.** When Simon the magician offered to buy the power of the Holy Spirit (Acts 8), Peter rebuked him saying, "Your money perish with you, because you thought that the gift of God could be purchased with money! You have neither part nor portion in this matter, for your heart is not right in the sight of God" (Acts 8:20,21).

4. **Misrepresenting the true character of God in the person of Jesus Christ.** Anyone portraying God as a cruel, harsh judge without compassion practices "seduction of Christianity." Jesus came to heal, set free from bondage and restore God's creation by establishing His Kingdom on earth as it is in heaven. Likewise, the Church has the same commission in the world today. "Love has been perfected among us in this: that we may have boldness in the day of judgment; because as He is, so are we in this world" (1 John 4:17).

5. **Exercising a spiritual office outside of God's calling upon one's life.** The Bible repeatedly records God's judgment upon people moving in spiritual offices under their own authority. God's Word gives precise instructions on offering sacrifices and administering sacraments. God never ignores violations of spiritual laws. Correction of senior pastors over major ministries is proper only by designated spiritual elders to the general Church. The anointed power of God designates leadership within the body of Christ. People do not choose spiritual leaders. God's Word teaches, "And whosoever exalts himself will be abased . . ." (Matthew 23:12). "Therefore humble yourselves under the mighty hand of God,

the way we get authorized

121

that He may exalt you in due time" (1 Peter 5:6). I believe this violation of spiritual authority is a major transgression and "seduction" of Christianity.

6. **Failing to demonstrate and communicate unity in the body of Christ.** Causing division among believers is clearly "seduction" of Christianity. Jesus' prayer for unity (John 17) exposes those who work counter to God's will in the body of Christ. I understand the concern of those who equate promoting "unity" with humanistic "one world government." But in our recognition of error, let us also admit that God intends that the government of the world "... be upon His (Jesus') shoulder" (Isaiah 9:6). One world government is God's plan under the reign of Jesus Christ, the King, to whom "every knee shall bow ..." (Philippians 2:10). Let me underscore my belief that this government will not be realized on earth until Christ returns.

7. **Failing to present the "gospel of the Kingdom."** The gospel of Jesus Christ is good news! The gospel of Christ is the most liberating, healing, life-giving truth that the world has ever heard. Christian teachers designating themselves as self-appointed critics, assigned to inspect ministries and ministers, are not promoting the gospel of Jesus Christ. They sit in "Moses' seat," judging in the spirit of the Pharisees. The good news of the Kingdom overcomes darkness with light, evil with good ... (Luke 4:16-19).

8. **Attempting to bring one under someone's power or influence by force or oppression.** This "seduction" applies on every level of human interaction—from one-to-one relationships, to religious systems, to oppressive governments. Any form of personal, religious or political oppression is the "seduction" of Christianity. Spiritual truth is a liber-

ating force, freeing people to choose righteousness and God's will. Truth sets us free (John 8:32).

9. **Polluting the natural environment instead of caring for the earth as good stewards.** Man depends upon the earth for life. The earth is the Lord's (Psalm 24:1). Redemption applies as much to the earth as to human souls. In fact, redemption returns all of creation to its original state when God pronounced it "good" in the Garden of Eden. God promises that repentance from sin and humbling ourselves in prayer will cause Him to "hear from heaven and heal our land" (2 Chronicles 7:14). "Seduction" of Christianity promotes a disregard for ecological concerns as an integral part of the gospel.

10. **Promoting a spirit of judgment instead of love in the Church.** Any believer who stirs up attitudes of suspicion and judgment in the Church is practicing "seduction" of Christianity. If I did not personally know the spirit of many of the ministries under attack today in the media, I would be guarded toward receiving their messages. My prayers for God's blessings upon them would be lost. Lacking spiritual unity with these ministers as brothers and sisters in the Lord weakens the total witness of the Church as one in Christ.

11. **Substituting natural talent for true gifts from God.** Whenever God-given talent is used in worldly pursuits for one's personal ambition or gain, or someone's natural talent is substituted for the anointing of God in ministry, that prostitution of gifts becomes "seduction" of Christianity. David was gifted on the harp. He was also skillful with the slingshot. David used both "talents" as spiritual weapons to bring honor to the Lord. Gideon was called "a man of valor" because God could trust him

to lead His army in obedience to God's commands.

12. **Attacking true revelation from God by persuading people to accept the "teaching and traditions of men."** Christian leaders who adhere to human traditions or structures which conflict with the move of the Holy Spirit among God's people practice "seduction" of Christianity. Jesus asked the Pharisees, "Why do you also transgress the commandment of God because of your tradition?" Then Jesus quotes Isaiah, ". . . teaching as doctrines the commandments of men . . ." (Matthew 15:3,9; Isaiah 29:13).

13. **Rejecting the incarnation of Jesus Christ and the Church as the on-going incarnation of Christ in the earth.** God, the Holy Spirit, is alive and at work in God's people around the world today. The body of Christ is Christ's eyes, ears, mouth, hands and heart to minister to the world just as Jesus did. To reject the teaching of "God in the flesh" surfaces the antichrist spirit in the world (1 John 4:2,3).

14. **Rejecting God's true authority by unbelief.** Jesus could do no miracles among His own people because of their lack of belief. They had a "Nazareth mentality" toward Jesus, the carpenter's son, and refused to see Him as God's chosen voice to bring them to Kingdom comprehension (Luke 4:22-27). Unbelief, or the attempt to prevent others from believing in God's voice to His people is "seduction" of Christianity.

15. **Withstanding ordained spiritual authority.** The examples in Scripture of those attempting to destroy God's appointed vessels are numerous, but the spiritual consequences of such attempts are absolute laws of God—Aaron and Miriam's murmuring

against Moses, Saul's pursuit of David, Daniel in the lions' den, Peter's release from prison as the Church prayed . . . God clearly warns, "Do not touch My anointed ones, and do My prophets no harm" (1 Chronicles 16:22). I intercede before God for those who attack called ministers of the Lord today.

16. **Restricting anyone from service to God on the basis of sex, education, marital status or social standing.** Anyone who judges those whom God has called into ministry based on social position violates New Testament principles. The same spirit that promoted a tug-of-war in the early church over the Jews' and Gentiles' rights as citizens of the household of faith still invokes controversy today. Now we focus on gender, marital status and ordination certificates. The arguments of prejudice and judgment are the same (Romans 2:1-11).

17. **Combining Christian teaching with worldly philosophies.** One of the most obvious examples of this "seduction" of Christianity is Liberation Theology which is now sweeping throughout Latin America. The foundation of this theology is Marxism, not God's Word. The goals of Liberation Theology, though steeped in spiritual ideologies, are basically humanistic. This "theology" is far more politically motivated than spiritually liberating. Whereas the new birth in Jesus Christ changes one from the inner man so that he influences his society, Liberation Theology proposes changing society to influence men. Such theology is humanistic, not Christian. It will never work! God will not allow mixture of carnal and spiritual in accomplishing His purposes. ". . . flesh and blood cannot inherit the kingdom of God . . ." (1 Corinthians 15:50). We must move according to the leading of the Holy Spirit. ". . . 'Not by might nor by

power, but by My Spirit,' says the Lord of hosts"
(Zechariah 4:6).

18. **Promoting one's own interest or projects
among Christian people.** Too many "Christian"
writers, artists, singers, etc., are traveling the Christian circuits promoting their projects. They mer-
chandise their own talents and rob God's people of
ministry according to His Word and His will. Their
interests focus on self-aggrandizement, royalty
checks, personal notoriety and influence. Unfortu-
nately, many sheep fall prey to their schemes.

Correcting The Errors of Seduction

Allow me to share five ways in which the Church
can effectively correct the errors of "seduction" of
Christianity.

1. **We must follow God's Word in bringing correction to those who offend us.** Personal contact
with those who we believe are teaching error is essential in godly correction. An adequate witness is required to confirm an offense. Acts 15 offers guidelines to peacefully bringing reconciliation to the
Church.

2. **God's people must begin to submit willingly
to called and proven eldership in the body of
Christ.** Ministries are judged by their fruit. Eldership offers protection, covering and discernment in
seeking direction for God's people.

3. **The Church must enter into dedicated intercession for brothers and sisters who are teaching error.** A spirit of reconciliation is essential in
healing the wounds of the Church. Only prayer
brings us into a spirit of forgiveness, compassion and
grace. Prayer assures results. Paul admonishes,
". . . you who are spiritual restore . . . lest you also be

126

tempted" (Galatians 6:1).

4. We must end public attacks against one another **in order to witness the gospel of Christ to the unsaved world.** Let spiritual people solve their differences behind closed doors. Those who name the name of Jesus must speak as one voice if we are to impact the world with the gospel of the Kingdom as Jesus commanded us to do. The secular press enjoys inner church conflicts. Our arguments with one another weaken our confrontations against world systems. More press coverage was given to arguments between conservative and moderate theologians in a certain denomination recently at their convention in Atlanta, than over any positive decisions that those Christians made at their gathering.

5. We must remember that the spirit of Christ **is always the spirit of recovery and reconciliation.** The story of the prodigal son gives insights into the spirit of Christ toward those who get into trouble. The Spirit of God opens His arms to all who repent. After the resurrection, Jesus specifically asked for Peter, who had denied the Lord in fear of what people would say and do if they knew he had been with Jesus. But Jesus did not give up on the disciple because of His mistakes (Mark 16:7).

Many levels of truth are contained in the simplicity of God's Word, and especially in Christ's teachings. Truth is seldom derived by giving a simple "yes" or "no" answer to some question or situation. The scribes and Pharisees tried repeatedly to trap Jesus with their questions. Jesus always addressed the hearts and motives of His listeners in the answers He gave to them. Uncovering a brother's sin is always seductive.

While some people spend all their efforts in exposing others for alleged "wrongs," I believe that God's heart searches the earth for protectors of those things which are "right." We need Kingdom protectors today who will give their lives to assure the safety of the Kingdom message and confront anyone who intends to harm it.

Miriam risked her own life to save her brother. That Hebrew baby lying in a basket, breaking the law of the land because he was alive, floated along the banks of the Nile River to the safe protection of Pharaoh's daughter. Inside that basket lay the one who would be the solution to Hebrew bondage. Moses' life was spared because his mother took a risk in constructing a basket for him. His older sister stood watch over him until God intervened to save his life.

Likewise, an angel warned Joseph in a dream to take Jesus to Egypt because of Herod's attempt to kill "the King of the Jews." The Son of God was once a dependent little baby entrusted to a peasant carpenter and his young wife. Mary and Joseph served as protectors of the Kingdom, cooperating with God's plan for the world in practical, daily protection of His "Word in flesh" entrusted to them.

Mary's concern at becoming separated from her twelve-year-old son on their trip to the temple in Jerusalem involved far more than a mother's normal anxiety in that situation. Mary knew her son's identity. She was called by God to protect a little boy who was God's plan for redeeming "that which was lost" through the sin of man. Mary had to cooperate with God by humanly, naturally protecting God's provision for the world.

Protectors of the Kingdom understand the mission of the Church. Error is exposed when we discern what is and is not God's plan. As protectors of the Kingdom cooperate with God, His miraculous intervention in our behalf presses against the very gates of hell. Kingdom protectors will quiet the storms of controversy. And in obedience and faith, they will sound the trumpet proclaiming, "The Kingdom of God is at hand!"

8

LITTLE GODS

When a pastor is attacked in print by Christian writers who have quoted him out of context, he must remember that whether he likes them or not, he is still in covenant with them. I asked the Lord recently, "God, are you telling me that those who would say to the members of my church, 'Don't go to his church' and publicly call me a 'false prophet' are in covenant with You? Do you mean that I am in covenant with them, also?"

God answered me by speaking to my spirit, "Let's suppose you had five children. They began to fight among themselves. Perhaps one even killed another. They are still your children. Battles rage among My children today. Your actions toward them may change their perspective."

I replied, "God, let me hear it! Let me not use the same tools and weapons that they use. Let me express Your image. Allow me to express Your love, showing Your character, not being like a "little god" who judges and takes his own dominion."

At times of feeling hurt and weak I have thought, "But God, think what I could do in court proving defamation of character. My case would be so easily won!" Then the Spirit of the Lord replies, "Hold it a minute! Do you trust Me? Are you going to be a 'little god,' or are you going to be 'in My image?' " That question is the bottom line of solving the issues of controversy in the Church today. Some people have never learned the difference between the error of being a "little god" instead of living as one created "in His image." Are we really living as expressions of God's love?

We stand as the expression of God Who so loved us that He gave His son to die for us. We must learn how to enter into His vicariousness by forgiving, turning the other cheek and laying down our lives for His purposes. I've got news for Satan. He can never win when we use that strategy in warfare. When our spirits please God, the very issues where we battle often lead to greater enlightenment into the meaning of His Word. Endurance brings rewards. Jesus learned obedience through the things He suffered (Hebrews 5:8). We are conformed to "the image" of Christ as we forgive and love our persecutors—even in the heat of battle.

Time is on God's side. The Word of God teaches that the "devil knows his time is short." The onslaught of controversy in the Church today only

stresses the urgency of demonstrating Kingdom righteousness, peace and joy in the midst of a society in
chaos and a Church inflicting wounds against itself.
We read that "the earnest expectation of the creation
eagerly waits for the revealing of the sons of God"
(Romans 8:19). This "revealing" or "manifestation"
simply means demonstrating responsible Christianity to the extent that we witness as "salt" and "light"
to the world. Our lives witness that obedience to God
works better than humanistic goals. Jesus Christ has
redeemed us from the power of sin and disobedience
to give us the power to live victoriously in Christ.

Evangelist Jimmy Swaggart quoted me extensively
in an article claiming that I (and others) teach that
the world will get better and better until everyone on
earth is a Christian, and then Christ will return. I
have never taught that, nor do I know of any
orthodox Christian ministry that does. I do believe
that Christians will demonstrate the Kingdom of God
as a witness in every area of life before Christ
returns. Peter preached on the day of Pentecost,
". . . whom (referring to Jesus Christ) heaven must
receive **until** the times of restoration of all things,
which God has spoken by the mouth of all His holy
prophets since the world began" (Acts 3:21).

In every world system—arts, politics, finance, education, sports, etc.—God shines His light of truth
through disciples whom He calls "the light of the
world" and the "salt of the earth." Christians today
should be saying to their society, "This is the way;
walk ye in it . . ." Many people will respond to their
witness and others will reject it. All will be forced to
make a choice between a kingdom of darkness and
the Kingdom of light.

Critics of "Kingdom Age" teaching [Swaggart's

term] focus primarily on one accusation: man's view of himself as a "little god." They point out that instead of one living in God's enlightenment and truth, man becomes a god unto himself. In his article, Evangelist Swaggart quoted me, a quote which Dave Hunt also wrote in *Seduction of Christianity,* concerning ". . . God has little gods . . ." I never intended the connotations which these writers assign to that statement. I have never taught their conclusions of the statement's meaning to my congregation at Chapel Hill Harvester Church in Atlanta. Any member of my congregation, chosen at random, would verify the error in their assumptions of the quote's meaning.

I wish now to differentiate between man's view of himself as a "little god," as opposed to his being created "in the image of God." These perspectives are quite opposed. A "little god" exalts man. One created "in the image of God" exalts, expresses or magnifies the Lord. Let me assure the critics of Kingdom teaching that the essence of the Kingdom of God establishes Jesus as King and Lord over all creation in heaven and earth. Jesus is King of the Kingdom—we are His subjects, a royal priesthood unto Him, living daily in preparation to rule and reign with Him.

The greatest confusion among evangelicals who recognize that the Spirit of God is moving in great power among His people today is understanding the parameters of man's "dominion" under God. God is sovereign. Critics of ministries teaching Christians to pursue "dominion" are correct in pointing out the dangers of man's even attempting to become "like God." In this regard, I appreciate aspects of Dave Hunt's extensive warnings that man, like Satan, can become proud and lift himself to a place of self-aggrandizement that God never intended. The critics are wrong, however, in their failure to understand that God gave dominion to man for the correction of chaotic conditions on planet earth.

Then God said, "Let Us make man in Our image, according to Our likeness; let them have dominion over the fish of the sea, over the birds of the air, and over the cattle, over all the earth and over every creeping thing that creeps on the earth. So God created man in His own image; in the image of God He created him; male and female He created them." (Genesis 1:26,27)

Satan's attempt to be "like God" resulted in the world becoming a dark, formless void. In the midst of that void, God created a garden and placed man in it as its proprietor. Those crying "seduction" in the Church do not acknowledge the difference between being created "in the image of God" and being "like God." A "like God" spirit always challenges God's authority. He says, "God, You are not fair! I know my rights! I don't care what Your Word says for me to do; I'll make my own decisions!"

"How you are fallen from heaven, O Lucifer, son of the morning! How you are cut down to the ground, you who weakened the nations! For you have said in your heart: 'I will ascend into heaven, I will exalt my throne above the stars of God; I will also sit on the mount of the congregation on the farthest sides of the north; I will ascend above the heights of the clouds, I will be like the Most High.' " (Isaiah 14:12-14)

Lucifer tried to give the woman the same ambition that caused him to fall. He said, "God knows that in the day you eat of it your eyes will be opened, and you will be like God, knowing good and evil" (Genesis 3:5). The underlying message was, "It is desirable to make you wise. Now you will not be subject to the

Father, but you will exert another authority in your own image. You can make your own decisions. You will be **like God,** a ruler yourself without needing headship."

Dave Hunt is correct in saying that a "like God" spirit has infiltrated the Church. I disagree with him, however, on some of the ministries he says are the sources of this infiltration. "Faith," "dominion" and "the Kingdom of God" are all orthodox, biblical concepts. Every Christian accepts these concepts as being theologically sound. However, many Christians accept Kingdom teaching only as long as it remains theoretical. The fear of Mr. Hunt and some other teachers is the demonstration of Kingdom concepts. Applied Christianity, calling for supernatural interaction of man and God to accomplish God's will, is threatening to people who read the Bible with rigid dispensationalist's views.

Faith lived out, for instance, often calls for unreasonable actions. Peter's walking on the water toward Jesus was an unreasonable act of faith. When the disciple noticed the wind and waves and began to realize how impossible his actions were, he sank. Jesus asked him, "Why did you doubt?" It's true that some people carry the concept of "faith" to extremes by attempting to use faith to please themselves. "Name it and claim it" extremes are an abuse of Christian faith. So how do we confront the possibility of error in order to enjoy the benefits of being created "in the image of God"? The Bible tells us to discern the spirit!

People with a "like God" spirit always desire to move beyond their callings. They exalt themselves in their own wisdom. Like Eve, they want to decide for themselves what is "good" or "evil." They reject

God's Word as the standard for righteousness by justifying their own self-seeking goals. Success is judged by worldly standards, based on one's possessions or intellectual achievement. "Like god" spirits seek things, not the God of things Who prospers them according to His will. Who was more prosperous: the man riding in golden chariots, spending money on wining and dining people, or the Apostle Paul writing in prison, "I can do all things through Christ who strengthens me" (Philippians 4:13)?

The conflict between spirits who try to be "little gods" and those who are created "in the image of God" is as ancient as the fall of mankind. God desired a sacrifice from Cain and Abel. He wanted their firstfruits, the finest offering they had. Abel chose a lamb without blemish to give to God. Abel was filled with joy. He went skipping down to the field saying, "I'm so glad I can bring my best offering to God. God is my Helper and my Keeper. He is the One Who keeps me from being lonely. He is the One Who can give me answers and a purpose in life."

Cain reasoned within himself, "After all, I'm the one who needs to prosper. I'll give vegetables to God. What's the difference? My sacrifice looks as good as Abel's." While Abel concentrated on pleasing God, Cain decided to give a sacrifice that made sense to him. The "little god" became so incensed with his brother's obedience to God's direction that he killed Abel. That fleshly reaction toward people of spiritual obedience is consistent throughout the history of mankind. The sons of the flesh inevitably persecute the sons of the Spirit.

The nation of Israel demanded a king, and so God instructed the prophet Samuel to anoint Saul. God ordered Saul to go to a certain wicked city and destroy everything in it. Saul began to reason within himself. He listened to the people instead of to God. Rather than destroying everything, he decided to save some of the fruit and herd to use as sacrifices to God (1 Samuel 15:10-35).

A "like God" spirit always challenges God's direction. They say, "God, You don't know what is best. You really don't understand that my situation is an exception to Your commands." They become wise in their own conceits. They may look, sing or act religious, but they follow the gods of this world to please themselves.

Christians with spirits expressing the "image of God" recognize that obedience is God's covenant requirement. We may not even fully understand the reasons for God's commands, but we follow Him willingly. God said to Abraham, "I'm in covenant with you. I want you to give Me your son." Now Abraham was in such a binding covenant with God, that God later issued that same command upon Himself. When God said to Abraham, "Give Me your son," God was also saying, "I will give My Son for the sake of the world."

Abraham demonstrated the "image of God." He said, "God, I don't understand! You promised to give me this son! His birth was miraculous. You said that my seed would be like the stars of the heavens. But God, You said to do it. I don't understand, but I will obey Your voice." Yes, Abraham obeyed in blind obedience. Yes, Abraham obeyed God without knowing the reasons for God's command. Abraham, the father of the household of faith, lived as a man who understood that he was created "in the image of God."

The "image of God" is fully demonstrated in the life of Jesus Christ. Jesus' actions were the epitome of the Father's will. He said to His disciples, "Have I been with you so long, and you haven't seen the Father?" Jesus Christ is the express image of God. "... who being the brightness of His glory and the express image of His person ..." (Hebrews 1:3). "He is the image of the invisible God, the firstborn over all creation" (Colossians 1:15). "For in Him dwells all the fullness of the Godhead bodily; and you are complete in Him, who is the head of all principality and power" (Colossians 2:9,10).

Jesus' obedience to God took Him to the cross. He obeyed God in healing the sick and setting people free from bondage. Everything Jesus said and did expressed the image of His Father. If we know Jesus, we know the Father. Likewise, Jesus intends for the world to know Him because they know His Church. The Church is the express "image" of Christ in the world. Repentance means rejecting the desire to be "like God" with human selfishness, aggression, greed and ambition. As new creations, old things (including thought processes) pass away and, behold, all things (thoughts that please the Lord) are new. In His image, we think the thoughts of God; we live out the life of Christ in our own lives.

We are in this world just as Jesus was in this world (1 John 4:17). To understand the "image of God," we must live out the character of God in the world. God is love. Jesus Christ is love. Since we are the body of Jesus Christ, we are also motivated by love, not because we become a "little god," but because we follow the Spirit. We become the expression of God's love and restoration to others.

Perhaps Christians respond to the idea of being "in the image of God" by saying, "But my flesh is weak!" So was David's and Paul's. Paul admitted that the things he wanted to do, he wasn't able to accomplish. Things he didn't want to do, he found himself doing. But he affirms, "In my spirit, I have found victory in Christ" (1 Corinthians 7:14-25 & 8:1,2). The wretched man, controlled by a "little god" spirit, is only set free by the resurrection power of Christ. Through Christ, we are able to follow the leading of the Holy Spirit (Romans 8:3-10).

When the prophet confronted David concerning his sin, David immediately responded by saying, "You're right, and I'm wrong!" David said to Nathan, "I don't need any further explanation. I alone have sinned against God" (2 Samuel 12:13). No biblical writer better demonstrates exaltation to God than David expresses in the Psalms. In spite of weaknesses in the flesh, David's spirit soared with an ability to magnify God in the midst of persecution and suffering as well as in gratitude for God's blessings. Many of the Psalms begin with complaints over David's circumstances, but before he finishes crying out to God, his spirit begins to worship the Lord.

The reason for giving the Holy Spirit at Pentecost was to help us live "in the image of God." The Holy Spirit prevents us from becoming "little gods" unto ourselves. God's anointing and power brings to bear the authority of God in our lives. God-given authority produces the image of God within us. That authority confronts sin within us individually. Then God's authority in our lives begins to witness against world systems and challenges oppressive kingdoms of this world. Jesus said, "All authority has been given to Me in heaven and on earth. Because I am going to give you that authority, I want you to disciple all nations" (Matthew 28:18-20).

Recently a television evangelist stated that God is

not concerned about nations. He said that God is only concerned about "preaching the gospel to every creature." I challenge that statement as being unscriptural. God gives us the commission, the authority and the power to disciple all nations (Matthew 28:19). God intends for the Church to be "salt" and "light" to government officials, the kings and judges who govern our world. God is concerned about government.

The voice of the Church stands as Samuel stood between the kingdoms of Saul and David. Samuel and Nathan were not kings, but they represented God's voice to government leaders. Today God is saying to His people, "I want you to move into those areas of influence and boldly speak My Word. According to My will, change the quality of life for My people."

How can we demonstrate this authority without the prophetic voice in the Church today? I was wrongly judged because someone quoted a passage out of my book, *The Wounded Body of Christ*. They totally missed the intent of the book which promotes healing and forgiveness among believers. On national television, they discussed one sentence in which I stated that ". . . prophets are not to be judged." Nobody judged Elijah, Amos or John the Baptist except God. The only proof of a true prophet is when his prophesies align people with God's will. A true prophet's message always comes true. God eliminates false prophets through death—either physical death or the "death" of their ministries.

In the paragraphs preceding the passage they quoted, I carefully explained the spirit of prophecy and how it works in the Church. Of course I believe that elders must judge the prophecy of one speaking

141

in an assembly. But many Christian critics are not concerned with fairness in making their accusations. Judging prophecy according to 1 Corinthians 14:29 refers to the "weighty matters" of the prophecy which must be judged by spiritual elders. But no man judges a prophet.

The subject of prophecy also called for an explanation of the difference between the "milk" of the Word and solid food—the "meat" of the Word of God. Anyone who can read will understand and comprehend God's written Word—even the newest Christian or a carnal mind. Their understanding of the Bible is the "milk" of the Word. "Milk" is easily digested or understood. The "meat" of the Word is the revelation of God and requires spiritual enlightenment by the Holy Spirit. The mysteries of God are the meat of the Word (1 Corinthians 2:14 and 1 Corinthians 3:2). Jesus told the disciples, "I have many more things to say to you, but when the Spirit comes, He will reveal those things to you."

Jesus said to Peter, "Flesh and blood has not revealed this to you, but My Father Who is in heaven . . ." He was referring to spiritual meat, an understanding of truth by revelation of God. The Church today moves into a crucial time in which we need understanding of God's Word by the enlightenment of the Holy Spirit. As the Church matures, God will bring us into a more complete comprehension of His Word.

Five qualities are essential for Christians to live "in the image of God." **First, we must realize that we are people under God's command.** We cannot live "in His image" unless He directs our thoughts, goals and actions. Jesus is our example, as One who lived in perfect harmony with God's direction for His life. We are under command of God's laws, His words, His structure and His design. We don't choose our family members—He does. We don't have options on whether we decide someone is worthy to be a brother or sister, or whether we like them, or approve of their behavior. If they are born into the family of God, they are part of us and we are part of them.

The second quality of living "in the image of God" is the ability to hear and know His voice. Jesus said, "My sheep hear My voice" (John 10:27). Spiritual growth is not determined by emotions, desires or achievements. Spiritual growth is the process of knowing and following God's voice. God's voice never caters to selfish desires of people. God's direction does not make us aggressive or ambitious except in dedication to please the Lord.

The third quality of living in "the image of God" is to become spiritual people. By "spiritual" I mean that we move beyond carnal decisions that satisfy our appetites. We walk by the Spirit in daily decisions and choices. We discern truth and follow it. Spiritual people live by the meat of God's Word.

Jesus taught important spiritual principles. Some people listened to Him teach and believed He was talking about something else, or just telling stories. For instance, Jesus said, "Destroy this temple, and in three days I will raise it up" (John 2:19). He was referring to His death and resurrection. Paul described the relationship between a man and his wife, and then admitted that he was actually speaking of Christ and the Church (Ephesians 5:22-32).

We need spiritual teachers in our day to discern the needs of the body and minister truth (Matthew 16:3). Some of the critics warring against my ministry say that we should never allow "private interpretation" of God's Word. They suggest that when a preacher finishes preaching, everyone should sit down with his Bible at home, read the scripture passages and then decide for himself whether or not the preaching he heard was truth from God.

That action **is** private interpretation! God calls preachers and teachers in the Church. When we take our Bibles home, get on our knees and make our own decisions concerning the preacher's sermon, we decide the truth of God's anointing according to our own private interpretations. We disregard the anointing or fruit of a ministry. If everyone judges God's direction like that, why have churches at all? What is the purpose of callings in the five-fold ministry, especially pastors and teachers (Ephesians 4:11-15)?

I believe some teachers attempt to sound "humble" by inviting others to judge their messages. Such an invitation contradicts a confident anointing from the Lord. It inevitably produces an "uncertain sound" in the message. I want God, Who has called me to preach, to judge my obedience to Him in boldly proclaiming His Word. We live in a day of such subtle deception in the Church. We must learn how to develop spiritual ears, spiritual hearts and spiritual discernment. The Church must learn to be attentive to the messages of true prophets from God (Amos 3:6-8).

The fourth quality to live "in the image of God" is to have the mind of Christ. Let the mind of Christ rule our hearts (Philippians 2:5). A flesh mind tells us one thing and always thrusts us into a struggle between our wills and God's will. The mind of Christ brings us into peaceful submission to God. We may experience warfare in carrying out God's

144

will, but we know His direction with certainty. The mind of Christ brings compassion, love, understanding, longsuffering and peace. To live "in the image of God," the mind of Christ must rule our thoughts.

Finally, we take up a cross if we deny ourselves as "little gods" to take on the "image of God." We understand the garden experience of Jesus. Perhaps He said, "Father, I do not fully understand this sacrifice. I won't feel You there with Me. I will cry, 'My God, why have You forsaken Me?' But this is Your will and Your purpose in sending Me. Not My will, but Yours be done." The cross means self-denial for the sake of God's purposes. We cannot be "in the image of God" without taking up a cross and following Him.

Jesus said, "If anyone desires to come after Me, let him deny himself, and take up his cross, and follow Me" (Matthew 16:24). The cross is our purpose in the Kingdom of God. That cross is not always pleasant or joyful. Because the cross means obedience to God, we will carry it with joy. Paul's letter to the Philippians, written in prison, was filled with joy. Martyrs of the Christian faith through the centuries have died horrible deaths of torture while singing hymns and forgiving their captors.

A "little god" spirit asserts his own rights. One living in the "image of God" realizes that he has no rights except to serve the Lord. The Church has so misunderstood this truth. We lay claim to "our rights" without ever hearing Jesus say, "Follow Me." When the financial prosperity of Christians is used for extra cars, boats, cabins and houses instead of for "food in God's house," God is grieved (Malachi 3:10). We've totally failed to understand the principles of covenant with God. Too many Christians live to

145

serve their possessions. They assert their "rights" to be "little gods" over their ambitions.

God knows both the beginning and the end. He searches the thoughts and intents of our hearts. He prunes us and demands that we bear fruit in our lives. Whose kingdom do we express? Are we serving God's Kingdom or our own? When we flow in love, compassion and obedience to the Lord, we have confidence before God. Then we will minister in the anointing and power of His authority.

I often explain God's sovereignty and man's dominion over the earth as being like a father who gives the keys of the family car to his teenage son for the evening. That father sets parameters by which the son is allowed to use the family car. The father determines the time limits, the distance, and the proper use of that automobile. The son knows his dad's rules. He may violate those rules, but he faces the consequences of disobedience. He is trusted with his father's property and the use of that property. In a human example, that son could become a rebellious "little god" who drives as he pleases, or he may submit his will to use the family car with respect for his father's wishes—conforming his behavior to "his father's image."

God searches for people whom He can trust. The Bible says that He wants to show Himself strong in our behalf. When we are in covenant with God, He will "prepare a table before us in the presence of our enemies." He will "anoint our heads with oil." We need not fear attacks from the enemy or the accusations of men. God always wins, and He promises that those who live "in the image of God" will not be put to shame.

9

PROCLAMATION

In March 1986 I participated in a leadership conference in Washington, D.C. In the early morning as I contemplated my address to that conference, I looked out my hotel window at our nation's Capitol. I heard a familiar voice speaking in my spirit.

God spoke distinctly that the time has come for the Church to issue a proclamation of war against the spirits of atheism, lawlessness and mammon which grip our world. As I listened to God's direction, I realized how significantly these three spirits hinder the fulfillment of God's will in manifesting His Kingdom on earth.

Earlier I had written an outline for the sermon I

planned to deliver under the title, "Let My People Go." On reviewing my sermon notes, I had mistakenly written the title, "Let My Spirit Go." I started to correct the word "Spirit" when the Lord spoke to me that the title, as I had written it, expressed the message He intended for me to speak to pastors and ministry leaders.

I met in closed session with Church leaders at the conclusion of that conference. As a result of our discussion, we planned strategy for a proclamation of prayer on July 4, 1986, at the Capitol in Washington, D.C., state capitols across the U.S., county courthouses, the Statue of Liberty in New York, the Vatican in Rome, and on the lawns of government buildings in numerous foreign nations. A designated leader at each site read the proclamation prayer, while other committed Christians joined in agreement. Pastor Tommy Reid from Buffalo, New York, wrote the prayer of proclamation.

I believe the proclamation, pronounced around the world on July 4th, sounded an alarm in both heaven and earth that the war against oppressive spirits has reached a new dimension. Christians at government buildings in over sixty-five foreign countries joined American intercessors at every state capitol in praying this proclamation. We received letters, pictures and videos of groups praying from around the world.

In Santiago, Chile, over a thousand prayer warriors sang as they marched down the city streets in the rain after praying the proclamation at the President's residence. In Nicaragua and Cuba pastors had memorized the prayer because of the danger of taking the written prayer into their countries. They had taught the proclamation to their congregations. The people gathered inside their churches to join together in agreement against these ruler spirits of oppression at noon on July 4th.

Since prayers of proclamation are so vital to the spiritual conquest of the Church, I believe we must make a distinction between prayers of proclamation and criticism surrounding the teaching of "positive confession." Few Bible teachers will defend the extreme view most critics attribute to "positive confession." Warnings of extremes in "faith teaching" frighten many Christians from speaking any words of authority over their circumstances. Yet Christians must confidently speak words of faith to impact the earth with God's will in heaven. The spoken word is a powerful instrument for producing both good and evil. God's Word declares that life and death are in the power of the tongue (Proverbs 18:21).

One of the most controversial issues that Dave Hunt raises in *Seduction of Christianity* focuses on "positive confession." Mr. Hunt is offended by those identified as "word of faith" teachers who encourage Christians to speak of their desires for things (especially material luxuries) that they believe God will give to them. The extreme teaching of "positive confession" has been labeled "name it and claim it," signifying that a Christian can have anything he verbally articulates and believes he will receive from God.

Mr. Hunt rightfully takes issue with extreme connotations in "faith teaching." Someone needs to warn Christians who think that spiritual manipulation in prayer could result in God's blessing them with a big bank account. Yes, God's Word says that He will give us "the desires of our hearts." But no "dream come true" is the result of merely saying certain words repeatedly or concentrating on a mental picture of a "new Mercedes." Viewing God as an omnipotent Santa Claus in the sky will never accomplish God's purposes for His Church on earth today. Such views are a total misunderstanding of the purposes of prayer and faith.

However, the problem with Dave Hunt's warnings are two-fold. First, Jesus repeatedly told His disciples that whatever they asked in His name, they would receive. He gave them authority in prayer, both in heaven and on earth by binding and loosing. He encouraged them to "speak to the mountain" to be removed and cast into the sea. Jesus Himself spoke words of deliverance, calmed the weather, cursed a fig tree and rebuked infirmities.

We must realize that Jesus expected His disciples to follow His example in ministry. It's important to note, however, that when His disciples were ready to "call down fire from heaven" to deal with people opposing Jesus' ministry, He rebuked them for their lack of spiritual understanding (Luke 9:54,55). Obviously, Jesus imposed restrictions on the disciples' aggressive presumptions in manifesting supernatural power in their proclamations.

Secondly, Dave Hunt associates the total positive confession message, attributed to the teachers whom God has called to bring an understanding of faith principles to the Church (Norman Vincent Peale, Robert Schuller, Charles Capps, Paul Yonggi Cho, Kenneth Hagin, Kenneth Copeland, etc.), with occult practices of visualization, mind power, repetitive chants, and human potential promoting man-centered theology. In this regard, Mr. Hunt has made a great error.

Again, Dave Hunt interprets the teaching of faith implementation through the eyes of an occult researcher and reacts to any similarities in the two perspectives without carefully discerning the differences. Many of his correlations and conclusions sound correct to one unfamiliar with these teachers. In that regard, Mr. Hunt opens the door to confusion within the body of Christ. Neither the teaching of Robert Schuller's "possibility thinking," nor Norman Vincent Peale's "positive thinking" promote occult practices, though admittedly extreme interpretations of their teaching could certainly mislead someone into believing that ". . . faith is not placed *in* God but is a power directed *at* God which forces Him to do for us what we have believed He will do" (Hunt, p.24,25). As the pastor of a large congregation, I can attest to the painful repercussions of such misunderstandings.

I believe that some clarity may be derived in redefining our terms. I teach that the Lord's Prayer is a prayer of proclamation. In fact, many of the scriptures often used by "faith" and "word" teachers, which set off alarms in Dave Hunt and others, are merely proclamations of God's will "on earth as it is in heaven."

Proclamations of God's will always ignite spiritual warfare. The spiritual enemies Jesus confronted are the same enemies we face today. Proclamations from God refute Satan's lies of defeat, despair and hopelessness. In order for God's people to issue a proclamation of "the acceptable year of the Lord" to our generation, we must first identify the enemies hindering the release of God's Spirit. We must use the spiritual weapons of warfare which Jesus gave to His Church to bind powers and principalities opposing God's plan. Since the Day of Pentecost, there has never been a more crucial time in history to loose the Spirit of the Lord to flow than now.

151

The keys of the Kingdom are loosing and binding in intercession, keys which unlock spiritual resources to manifest the Kingdom of God on earth in every area of life. Binding spirits of darkness releases the Holy Spirit to complete God's plan for the earth. Jesus said that the Kingdom of heaven "suffers violence" and "the violent take it by force" (Matthew 11:12). Christians are admonished "to press" toward the goal of our high calling. Paul instructed the Church to "put on the whole armor of God," to stand boldly against spiritual forces opposed to God's will.

In over forty years of ministry, God spoke as clearly as He has ever spoken to me that the time is now for His Church to "Let My Spirit Go!" Implementation of strategy in warfare requires mature spiritual comprehension. God is calling for prayer warriors to join together in binding ruler spirits of atheism, lawlessness, mammon, and others in a proclamation which will hasten kingdom confrontations both in heaven and on earth.

As the power of God is released in these areas, Christians must prepare for an increase in the kinds of disturbing events already erupting around the world. Spiritual warfare begins in the heavenlies. Remember, oneness with God in continuous intercession assures that we will have peace amid the storms of confrontations and individual tests. God desires to pour out His Spirit on His sons and daughters in these days. Often He lacks intercessors willing to move according to His command. God is searching the earth for men and women who are willing to agree with Him to see His will on earth and to move in obedience in implementing His direction.

Binding powers and principalities of darkness will "clean out the wells" of life, allowing the Spirit to flow. An interesting story in Genesis 26:12-22 tells of confrontations Isaac encountered in cleaning out the wells that his father, Abraham, had dug years earlier. The Philistines had clogged up the wells with dirt. They feared Isaac's power and influence, and they begged the man of God to move away from their land.

Instead of giving in and moving on, Isaac cleaned out the dirt. His work allowed water from those wells to become a source of life to his household. Today God is calling for His people to clean out the clogs of spiritual wells that they might flow in influencing politics, education, economics, the arts, sports and other worldly kingdoms. Only the flow of the Holy Spirit in these areas will reveal God's glory as a witness, or standard, to people living in darkness. Our witness in demonstrating God's will becomes the "yardstick" measure by which God will judge the world.

God may want to bless His people, but when we allow our wells to become cluttered with sin and self-gratification, His Spirit cannot flow. We cannot live as expressions of God to others. In order to release the Spirit of God to do His work, we must repent, forgive others and clean out our spiritual wells so living rivers can flow from us. By our witness we show the world the mind and will of the Father. We express the Father when we rejoice in the midst of tribulation. We obey God's direction in spite of criticism from other people whenever we love those who persecute us. God's Spirit will only be poured into vessels who are open to receive His life. Allow me to emphasize again that God's will is based on His Word. Spiritual proclamation is never self-seeking nor self-motivated. The fruit of a spiritual proclamation always brings

153

glory to God.

We hinder the flow of the Spirit unless we continuously pour out Spirit life from within us. Our capacity to love increases only as we love others by the Spirit. Our capacity to feel compassion increases as we minister restoration to those who have been wounded and bruised in turbulent situations of life. Our capacity to grow in faith increases only when we act according to the Holy Spirit's direction, believing God's Word in faith instead of following the mind of reason.

Yielding our wills to God determines the extent that God's power flows in our lives. "Let God arise and His enemies be scattered . . ." (Psalm 68:1). The word "let" indicates that we are given the choice of saying "yes" or "no" to the flow of the Spirit within us. " 'Let' not your hearts be troubled" indicates we control our emotional responses to life situations by choosing to follow either faith in God or fear in our circumstances.

We must "clean out the spiritual clogs" individually and corporately. When we obey God's command to "Let My Spirit Go," we offer our families, communities and society a distinct choice between God's will and secular thinking. As God's power is demonstrated through His people, we become visible witnesses or expressions of God. Unbelievers observe empowered Christian intercessors in numerous situations. They begin to recognize alternative attitudes to the money-motivated lifestyles which set standards in the world.

Jesus said that we are preserving "salt" and directive "light" to our society. For this reason, prayers asking God for "a new Mercedes" to impress people totally oppose the commission of Christ to be His witnesses. Is the prayer for "a Mercedes" ever God's will? Discern the spirit; test the motives; test the fruit. The material world must always serve the purposes of God in the spiritual realm. Possessions are not evil, but our response and attitude toward possessions often measure our spiritual values. Where are our hearts? The treasure of our lives is found either on earth or in heaven. That determination of our treasure is crucial in understanding intercessory proclamation.

Our obedience to God releases His power within us. Our primary goal in life is fulfilling Christ's commission to His Church: to live as witnesses to the good news of God's redemptive plan. This witness is lived out through example. Jesus Christ lived as the total expression of God in the world. Throughout Scripture, two witnesses were always required to establish truth. Now the Church stands with Christ as that second witness to powers and principalities, proving that God's plan works. We must listen to the Holy Spirit and move in obedience to His direction. Just as Jesus came to dethrone Satan by restoring "that which was lost," the Church must also be about the Father's business of overcoming world systems by faith, love and obedience.

Christians must learn God's strategy in waging warfare. Binding and loosing of spirits begins in the spiritual realm in heaven before we receive manifestations in the physical realm of our circumstances on earth. Job is a prototype of the Church in warfare. Job's integrity before God stood as a witness against Satan's authority in the world. Likewise, we are called to be such witnesses. Like Job, we may go through trials at times, but we cannot lose this war. Unity of spirits, joined in agreement on earth to accomplish God's will, always triggers confrontations with spiritual forces in the heavens. As the Spirit of God empowers His Church amid confrontations, believers begin to experience the reality of Christ's authority within His body on earth.

Christians never need to assert their authority in the manner that the Pharisees and publicans wielded the Law. We have been endued with the authority of Christ through the Holy Spirit. As His witnesses, we are the implementors of His will. The cross of Jesus Christ is lived out in us as we become God's expression of vicarious love in a hostile environment. The role of the Church depicts the expression of God's loving mercy at work in a spiritually oppressed society. The strategy of the cross—denying ourselves, meekness, forgiveness, unconditional love—will always defeat oppressive strongholds working against God's will.

Even the gates of hell cannot prevail against the Church moving in love and spiritual authority. Christians will storm the strongholds of Satan—the authority of world systems—by using the keys that God gave to us: the ability to bind and to loose. We can be God's expression only as we learn to use the keys of His authority through intercession. We never need to cry for authority that we already have! God gave the Church "power from on high" to use!

Binding ruler spirits opposed to God and loosing the Holy Spirit to flow in the earth will reverberate in toppling world systems. Any house built on a foundation of "sand" instead of built on "the rock" of Jesus Christ will surely fall (Matthew 7:26). Are we eager to see the economy of the world shaken? Are we willing to take a stand against public schools which pass rulings forbidding any mention of God in their textbooks? Are we willing to go to court when the legal rights of the Church are threatened? Are we prepared to administer justice when the perpetrators of lawlessness in government are exposed? Will we speak out against socioeconomic prejudices? Spiritual warfare demands social confrontations! Are Christians willing to pay the price of confrontations? Are we willing to be misunderstood and falsely accused? Jesus was, and so we must also be ready to count the cost to be fit for the Kingdom of God!

Powerful prayer flows only as a result of a close relationship with God. The Holy Spirit intercedes for us according to God's perfect will. In spiritual intercession, we share the heart of a loving God Who weeps over a groaning world. Of course God is compassionate. He cries at the results of sin. But God also weeps because of where His people are in the process of reconciliation and redemption of that which was lost.

Just as Jesus wept at the tomb of Lazarus, God weeps today in spite of knowing that the solution to conflicts in heaven and earth is forthcoming. God never questions the fact that He has ordained a plan that will eventually reconcile the world to Himself. But His plan requires witnesses to demonstrate His Word to powers and principalities. God searches for people who walk by faith and obedience.

Intercession of the Holy Spirit restores the communication with God which mankind lost in the Garden of Eden. Not only was communication with God lost, Adam lost identity as being created in God's image, the fruit of innocence, dominion and authority. Man was created to walk with God in intimate fellowship. We enter again into that close relationship with God through continuous interaction with Him to accomplish His eternal purposes. This relationship is the basis of true intercession—a continuous walk with God, sharing His concerns and His perspective in every circumstance of life. Please note that I do not mean that man in his present state can become sinless or reach perfection. The total redemption of man will occur only at the return of Jesus Christ to rule and reign.

Prayer activates the will of God within us. In intercession we prepare our lives to express the mind of God. When the Holy Spirit has revealed the mind of the Father to God-called apostles and prophets, the body of Christ will know the areas in which they should release spiritual energy in intercession and faith.

God is raising up prayer warriors like Dr. Larry Lea to call the Church to intercession. This is the day for Christians to proclaim a "certain sound" of the trumpet to the world. The Church says confidently, "We know God's will because we are expressions of the Father." Is that a presumptuous statement? What else should the Church say? Jesus told His disciples, "If you've seen Me, you've seen the Father." Many people speak the mind of Satan, but only the Church moving in God's authority, according to His Word, can speak the mind of God. Paul said, "But we have the mind of Christ" (1 Corinthians 2:16).

True intercession by the Holy Spirit brings believers to the bold proclamation of God's will. Speaking "words of faith" with confidence only grows from the covenant relationship we share with God. Abraham, the father of the household of faith, held firmly to the bold promises of God though they were impossible, ridiculous promises according to his natural understanding. The biblical prophets proclaimed God's

Word to His people at His command. As the Word was released, the prophets waited for blessings to flow or judgment to fall, according to people's response of obedience or rebellion to the proclamation. Jesus commissioned His disciples to proclaim His gospel of life and an eternal Kingdom to whoever received His message. Judgment or blessings always follow preaching of the gospel message.

Reaching the spiritual maturity of knowing the mind of the Father and knowing what the Spirit is saying to the Church calls for responsible Christianity. If we abdicate our responsibility to express God to the world, beginning with our families, friends and neighbors, we close them off from God's plan for their lives. Daily we must seek the direction of the Spirit as to how we can become channels through which God's authority is released.

Any Christian can make bold proclamations of faith according to God's will. Jesus' prayer which "taught us to pray" was a prayer of bold proclamation. The Lord's Prayer, our model prayer, is simply a proclamation of God's will.

In the Lord's Prayer, Jesus proclaims the identity of the Father; proclaims the Father's will for His Kingdom to be manifested in both heaven and earth; asks for "daily bread," which I believe is revelation for that day (Jesus said, "I have bread that you know not of . . ."); asks "forgiveness" from God, according to one's own responsibility in maintaining harmonious relationships; proclaims God's guidance, protection and "deliverance from evil"; and finally, proclaims God's omnipotence to accomplish the proclamation spoken by the Spirit.

Why have Christians believed that the essence of prayer was asking for things or giving God information? Why has "intercession" often consisted of emotional wailing, groaning and repetitious phrases? Most public prayers are spoken to the people listening to the prayer instead of to God, spoken many times for the same reasons that Jesus rebuked the Pharisees for the manner in which they prayed.

The mourning and wailing of the publican, often called "intercession," has little to do with prayer as it is taught in the Word of God. I believe the scripture describing Jesus weeping over Jerusalem is a portrait of God's weeping over the world He desperately loves. God's Spirit is touched as He hears the world groaning, just as He responded to the cries of His people in bondage in Egypt. But the essence of intercession is depicted in God's relationship with Adam before man's fall into sin separated him from God's presence. The essence of prayer—true intercession—is the oneness which Jesus shared with the Father.

Most long, repetitious prayers only exhaust the one praying so that he is finally willing to obey God. Agonizing prayers only bring the one praying into subjection to God's will, which has not changed because of anything we have said or done. Begging God for something never changes His mind. The one who has agonized endless hours finally says as Jesus did at Gethsemane, ". . . not My will, but Yours, be done" (Luke 22:42).

Praying must be something more than a state of agony. Jesus Christ was not that sort of expression of God at all. When He saw a crisis in someone's life, He dealt with it in the character of God. He dealt lovingly with the woman caught in the act of adultery. He healed the sick and diseased as God instructed Him to do. He saw the temple misused, and dealt strongly with those offending the purposes of His

Father's house.

True intercession is taking strong, affirmative action, righting society's wrongs and addressing people's problems as an expression of God's character. Many times we pray as if we are heard by God for our "much saying." We equate "super-spirituality" with the length of time we pray. If Satan can keep Christians in their own sanctimonious sanctuaries praying by the clock, we'll never demonstrate the Kingdom of God! Paul said to pray always in the Spirit as part of our spiritual armor (Ephesians 6:18). Of course we must designate times of prayer as well as pray on the run! Prayer is that continuous relationship with the Lord.

The total secret of prayer is focusing on Jesus Christ as our example, the Firstfruit, the One Whom we imitate. How does Jesus' example relate to the doing of God's will on earth? Praying is seeking and doing the will of the Father. Oneness with God is the basis of intercession. In oneness, the Father is one with the Son, and we are one with Jesus Christ. In oneness, we also demonstrate that Jesus and the Father are one.

Such misunderstanding has clouded the proclamation of unity within the Church! Unity does not mean open acceptance of anyone, anywhere, who says anything. Unity of Spirit can only be found in Jesus Christ. God pours out His blessings today on those who come together in unity through Christ.

In the fall of 1986, my ministry experienced the blessings of unity through our annual pastors' conference. Since we began having these conferences in 1982, most of the speakers and Church leaders coming to the conferences were interested in discussing "Kingdom" teaching. In 1986 we deliberately broadened the base of a "Kingdom" focus with speakers from diverse ministry perspectives, callings and views. I had no idea what would happen with such diversity in a conference setting. As a pastor who believes firmly in Jesus' mandate for spiritual unity in the Church, I felt excitement stirring inside me knowing that God would sovereignly move to blend the messages of all the speakers.

Over one thousand Church leaders from various denominations registered for the conference. We were privileged to host almost two hundred pastors from Latin America and the Caribbean, many who had come from war-torn nations, some who had faced imprisonment for their faith.

Pastor Larry Lea from one of the fastest growing churches in America, Church on the Rock in Rockwall, Texas, opened the conference on Sunday night. Larry Lea shared a vision (which he said according to Scripture means that he is a "young man") that God had given to him on the significance of the Lord's Prayer. He said that the highest calling from God is the call to pray in agreement with God's will.

The next evening, Pastor Luther Blackwell from Cortland, Ohio, reminded the delegates that the throne of God is built on righteousness and justice. He pointed out that prejudice is still prevalent within the Church. Admitting that many forms of prejudice must be addressed, he dealt specifically with racial prejudice. He asked, "Where are the black Oral Roberts' . . . the black Billy Graham's?" He emphasized that our racial barriers have not completely thwarted the move of God in the Church, but they have definitely inhibited what God really desires to do.

Then Pastor Blackwell related a vision that God

had given him. God had told him that He was going to raise up several black ministers to speak against factions within the total Church, not just the black church. Then, in great humility, Pastor Blackwell said that God had called him to be one of those ministers. At the conclusion of this stirring message, Oral Roberts came to the pulpit, visibly shaken. He said he had undergone similar persecution in his ministry as Luther Blackwell had described. He said that the message by Luther Blackwell was so timely because the time has indeed come for the Church of the Lord Jesus Christ to come together as one body . . . not a white church or black church, but a unified body of Christ.

In what we knew to be a historic consecration, Oral Roberts called Luther Blackwell forth to lay hands on him. Bishop John Meares, Pastor Tommy Reid, Pastor Moses Vegh, along with other ministers on the platform and I, joined in laying hands on Luther Blackwell. In spiritual agreement, we confirmed the ministry God had called him to serve.

Pastor Tommy Reid from Buffalo, New York, addressed the conference by explaining what the "Kingdom message" is really all about. He emphasized that for too long we have kept the message of the Kingdom of God inside our stained glass windows and our church walls. He exhorted the delegates to reach out to the world of industry, commerce, marketing and all worldly kingdoms with solutions from God that will bring change.

Gary North, one of the most prolific authors of our day, addressed the conference in the afternoon. Gary is a Reformed Presbyterian whose extensive research of the historic Church enables him to see where the Church has been, where it is today, and where it is going. He warned the delegates not to fight the historic theological clashes repeatedly, and to watch our language by saying what we mean and meaning what we say. He elaborated upon the "word battles" within the body of Christ.

Bishop John Meares from Washington, D.C., picked up where Luther Blackwell's message left off. As a white pastor of a great inner-city church with a predominantly black membership, he shared the rewards of obedience to God's direction of ministry without prejudice. He described some of the racial struggles his congregation had overcome through the years.

Jamie Buckingham, editor-at-large for *Charisma* and *Ministries Magazine*, writer of the *Buckingham Report* now incorporated in *Ministries Magazine*, renowned author, pastor and teacher from Melbourne, Florida, told the conference delegates that he was a "bumblebee," whose task was to cross-pollinate within the Church. He brought to Atlanta on his "wings," seeds from other ministries to leave with us, and to take what he gathered from us to other places. He remarked that some flowers in God's garden refused to accept others as flowers, and simply regarded them as *weeds*.

Jamie Buckingham pointed out that though we may disagree philosophically or even theologically, we still share a brotherhood in a single family with a mutual Father. We all have questions for which we seek answers, and we all must take our places within the body of Christ with great love and understanding. Love is that enduring quality that binds us together as brothers and sisters in Christ.

A demonstration of that love flowed in the message that Oral Roberts brought to the conference. Oral Roberts is truly an apostle of healing to the body of

Christ. As God called him to bring healing to natural bodies, he is now being used of the Lord to bring healing to the body of Christ, the Church. He shared how God had called him to heal people, both medically and supernaturally through the gifts of healing. He told us that the reason he had founded a medical school was to train bright, young minds to become medical healers in the world. These young people, when fully trained, could go to the uttermost parts of the earth to give healing both medically and divinely through the combined power of prayer and medical skill.

The Church must be able to blend God's resources to meet the needs of mankind. How important unity of our resources becomes to our witness! Atlanta '86 demonstrated the value and richness of diversity in unity. Historically, whenever people were oppressed, whether they were slaves or a minority suffering under the hand of a common enemy, the people closed ranks to withstand the oppression.

Within our society, groups such as "People For the American Way" headed by Norman Lear are beginning to attack the Church with slick, expensive media campaigns. They picture Jerry Falwell, Charles Stanley and Jimmy Swaggart as enemies of "freedom" who try to force their convictions on a progressive-thinking public. They provide a toll-free number to solicit funds from the public to fight the message of the Church. In another media advertisement, actor Tom Selleck says that he doesn't want to hear preaching against drugs because such moralizing is a "sledgehammer" approach to combat drug abuse. Isn't it time that we united in a bold proclamation of the gospel of Christ that the gates of hell cannot stop?

At the conclusion of the Atlanta '86 Conference, Bishop John Meares and I flew to Benin City, Nigeria, where I delivered the dedication address of a circular, 20,000 seat auditorium, now the third largest church in the world. That service packed approximately 23,000 people into the auditorium with over thirty thousand people standing outside unable to press into the building. Armed guards surrounded twenty-two heads of state in Africa who attended the service. One African king spoke the name of Jesus Christ publicly for the first time. This is the first time such a pronouncement from a government official was made in over twenty years. The openness and hunger for the gospel of the Kingdom was absolutely extraordinary! The opportunities to influence millions of people for Jesus Christ is within our grasp!

Archbishop Benson Idahosa, a remarkable servant of the Lord who has founded over 3,000 African churches in twenty-six years, asked Bishop Meares and me to share in the ordination of 486 pastors and several bishops who serve in those churches. I could weep in realizing the material abundance of our land compared to the needs of these ministers. Our resources can so easily supply the needs of ministries around the world to proclaim the message of the Kingdom. We have been given so much from God. So much is required from us in these days of harvest!

God is saying, "Let My Spirit Go" as a proclamation to the earth. Just as Jesus proclaimed the "acceptable year of the Lord," God is seeking proclaimers who will clean out the spiritual wells hindering the Spirit's flow. We are not waging carnal warfare. We are waging spiritual warfare by using the keys of binding and loosing. The cross is God's strategy. Love is His force. We must recognize that we can

166

never alter God's will through intercession. Instead, we must identify His purposes, get in step with His direction, and proclaim His solutions to the pain of a groaning world.

10

THE AGE TO COME

People are concerned about the future. No generation has faced the possibility of annihilation more squarely than ours. The race for more and greater nuclear arms makes political decisions personally relevant. What kind of world are we giving our children? How do we prepare them for the challenges ahead? Where do we find security for the future in such turbulent times?

Inevitably, religion becomes a refuge against harsh realities of this world. I use the word "religion" because, though many people seek truth today, deception abounds in our generation. Constance Cumbey, a lawyer, wrote a best selling book called *The Hidden*

Dangers of the Rainbow (Huntington House, 1983), exposing the teaching of the New Age Movement. Dave Hunt, a certified public accountant, has researched the occult extensively, as I have discussed. These writers are not theologians, but they have benefited those of us in the ministry with careful research and factual information on cult doctrines. Among other things, their research confirms that people are searching for answers. They raise questions which require Bible teachers to make certain we are being understood.

Let me emphasize again that the Bible teaches that factual information is not in the same realm of understanding as spiritual enlightenment. I know that statement may seem presumptuous, even arrogant to the mind of reason. Jesus faced Pilate, declaring that He was a king. "Pilate therefore said to Him, 'Are You a King then?' Jesus answered, 'You say rightly that I am a king. For this cause I was born, and for this cause I have come into the world, that I should bear witness to the truth. Everyone who is of the truth hears My voice' " (John 18:37).

Jesus lived His life in two realms. He walked, talked and ministered in the realm of this world. He used stories in His teaching that were common experiences of the people who heard Him. These stories explained life in an unseen, eternal realm. Jesus claimed that He only spoke and did whatever His Father instructed Him to do (John 8:28). That claim infuriated some of the people hearing Him, especially proud religious leaders. His earthly ministry exemplified a man living in a period of history, yet perfectly relating in vertical communication with omnipotent, omniscient, omnipresent God. The Son of Mary claimed His Father to be the Creator of heaven and

earth. He claimed to be the King of an eternal Kingdom. Those claims sentenced Him to death on the
cross.

Most Christians acknowledge the importance of
their vertical relationships with God. Born-again
people pray, follow biblical teaching and participate
to varying degrees in the work of a local church.
They realize that God's will in their lives is not fatal-
istic coincidence. Following God's will requires com-
mitments and choices to seek God's direction. As
people seek more of the reality of Christ's Kingdom,
they encounter more resistance to God's will in their
circumstances. Fulfilling God's will means enlisting
in a spiritual army. Christians with great desire to
serve the Lord know they accomplish nothing apart
from close, continuous interaction with Him. When
He issues orders to His soldiers, He ensures us of victory over spiritual forces opposing His will.

The unseen world that Jesus revealed to us is a
well populated Kingdom. Both good and evil spirits
reside in this unseen realm. They constantly engage
in battle over worldly events. Christians generally
accept that they are surrounded by unseen beings:
angels who are ministering spirits (Hebrews 1:14);
departed saints who form a great cloud of witnesses
(Hebrews 12:1); and powers and principalities of darkness (Ephesians 6:12). Scripture indicates that these
beings possess conscious knowledge of our lives.
They interact with us.

One of the distinctions between saved and unsaved
people is an awareness of good and evil beings in the
unseen world. When a Christian's name is registered
in heaven, he has spiritual authority and is recognized by the inhabitants of the spirit realm. Authority is based on God's standards. For that reason, the

prayers of a righteous man have great power (James 5:16). The Apostle Paul said:

> ... *we do not look at the things which are seen, but at the things which are not seen. For the things which are seen are temporary, but the things which are not seen are eternal. (2 Corinthians 4:18)*

Seventy disciples returned to Jesus with thrilling reports about the missionary journeys where He had sent them. They had taught Kingdom principles, healed the sick and delivered people from bondage. "We cast out demons in Your Name!" they exclaimed. Jesus' response to them was very interesting. He said, "Nevertheless do not rejoice in this, that the spirits are subject to you, but rather rejoice that your names are written in heaven" (Luke 10:20). Jesus' response that they should rejoice was not referring to the salvation of these disciples. He wanted them to realize that their names were registered in the realm of the spirit world. In Jesus' name, they were able to minister with spiritual authority.

An example of men casting out demons whose names were not registered in the heavenlies were the Sons of Sceva:

> *And the evil spirit answered and said, "Jesus I know, and Paul I know; but who are you?" Then the man in whom the evil spirit was leaped on them, overpowered them, and prevailed against them, so that they fled out of that house naked and wounded." (Acts 19:15,16)*

Christians who are registered in heaven know the power of their source of authority—their covenant relationship with God. They have surrendered their lives in obedience to God's commands. Such obedience to God in the lives of men living on earth threatens powers of darkness who control world systems. Covenant Christians are people whom the Bible calls "overcomers." They engage in constant warfare just as Jesus did. They persist in believing they will realize the prophetic promises of God which He made to His covenant people. Jesus proclaimed that the "gates of hell" would not overpower them.

Dave Hunt writes in *Seduction of Christianity* that some ministers teach a Christianized form of "sorcery." He warns Christians against teachers claiming miracles or prosperity from God. Mr. Hunt contends that such claims focus on fulfilling man's desires rather than God's. The writer cites leading ministries that urge Christians to transcend their circumstances by pressing with faith into the world to come. He believes these ministries use Christian language to teach veiled occult philosophies. Mr. Hunt implies that a focus on the Spirit realm leads Christians to sins of idolatry, seances and mysticism. Teachers emphasizing scriptures urging Christians to press toward the age to come are warned about cults promoting a utopian existence, a New Age of humanistic good will. Dave Hunt asks the question, "Why is this?" He answers by writing:

"It is because most Christians are so uninformed about occultism that they wouldn't recognize it except in its most blatant forms . . . The extent to which anti-Christian and even occult beliefs have been integrated into Christianity within the last few years is staggering, and this trend is now accelerating at an alarming rate" (Dave Hunt & T.A. McMahon, *Seduction of Christianity*, Harvest House Press, 1985, p.12).

I agree with many of the warnings Dave Hunt gives in regard to the occult, Eastern mysticism, witchcraft, the worship of demons and genuine cult practices. Evil powers are real. However, underlying Dave Hunt's warnings is a danger of hindering Christians from seeking the sacramental truths of God's Word. Jesus blesses people who "hunger and thirst for righteousness" (Matthew 5:6). People who seek first the Kingdom of God and its righteousness inevitably direct their thoughts beyond the tangible realm of life's realities. Without becoming "mystical," they live their lives in a conscious awareness of vertical interaction in an eternal, unseen realm.

Jesus stood as a man with one foot in His historical period of time, and the other foot in the age to come. Jesus' life demonstrated transcending this world to show us the Father. Likewise, Christians who seek first the Kingdom of God live in both vertical and horizontal dimensions. Our transcending consciousness affects our daily decisions and lifestyles, thereby revealing Christ's presence within us to the world. This horizontal dimension focuses on God's will for mankind, His unfolding plan for His Church in an historical conquest to overpower evil forces in rebellion against God. Christians "press," as Paul expressed it, from this present age of testings and trials in our circumstances toward "the goal[s] of our high calling[s] of God in Christ Jesus" (Philippians 3:14).

In the present world, people are confined to earthly bodies. Laws of the flesh, such as the principle of sowing and reaping, govern the quality and effectiveness of one's passage through historical time. This present age remains affected by the curse of sin and rebellion. Germs, disease, pestilence, famine and pollution are some of the results of the laws of sin and death that afflict a sin-filled creation. All creation longs for the age to come (Romans 8:22,23).

Spiritual warfare rages in both the horizontal and vertical realms as Christians aggressively press toward Kingdom demonstration on earth as it is in heaven. Covenant people press with birth pangs of travail in intercession to bring forth the will of God. Pressing does not come by humanistic dedication or efforts, but by obedience in carrying out God's will. God's will comes to earth as believers follow the leading of the Holy Spirit. However, God's will always conflicts with world systems, the law of sin and death and the mind of reason governing our present age.

The horizontal dimension of God's plan should never be confused with goals of the New Age Movement. The "world to come" is not the result of man's efforts or group alliances. Paul warns us to beware of the "false circumcision," any covenant achieving evil purposes through the exaltation of man's abilities (Philippians 3:2). He defines the "true circumcision" as those ". . . who worship God in the Spirit, rejoice in Christ Jesus, and have no confidence in the flesh . . ." (Philippians 3:3).

No flesh will glory at the culmination of all things, when Christ returns to complete the reconciliation of things both in heaven and in earth (Ephesians 1:10). Man's flesh always fails. Obedience to God ultimately wins, no matter how despairing circumstances may appear to be in the midst of tribulation.

Our responsibility in fulfilling God's plan demands reliance on the Holy Spirit's work within us. God has limited Himself to work through His Church to accomplish His will. God calls for people who are willing to give their bodies as "living sacrifices." He asks that we resist "being conformed to this world," but instead be "transformed by the renewing of our minds" (Romans 12:1,2).

A renewed mind seeks those things [rewards, relationships, goals, etc.] which are above [the age to come] rather than seeking gratification in this present age (Colossians 3:2-4). A renewed mind recognizes earthly relationships according to Kingdom purposes. Jesus even resisted the pressure of natural relationships. He fulfilled His calling from God as His first priority. He said, ". . . Who is my mother and who are my brothers? For whoever does the will of My Father in heaven is My brother and sister and mother" (Matthew 12:48, 50).

Historical time is ending. Worldwide conflicts, perplexities and natural calamities offer negative proof that time is running out. The positive evidence that we stand on the horizon of the age to come is that the Church is growing up. The bride is maturing (Galatians 4:15). She is beginning to come into unity of faith (Ephesians 4:13) and to speak with authority (1 Corinthians 13:11).

John reminds us that ". . . the world is passing away, and the lust of it; but he who does the will of God abides forever" (1 John 2:17). John is referring to the systems of this world which are passing away, not the physical planet which God created and loves (Psalm 24:1).

Christians who comprehend the horizontal and vertical realms of seeking first the Kingdom of God also recognize that they are no more subject to world systems than Jesus was. They are citizens of His Kingdom. Of course they obey the laws of society based on God's ordinances of peace and blessings within the social order (Roman 13:2,3). But their citizenship is registered in the spiritual realm. In this citizenship, the universal Church of Jesus Christ transcends historical time and national identification.

Paul said, "For our citizenship is in heaven, from which we also eagerly wait for the Savior, the Lord Jesus Christ, who will transform our lowly body that it may be conformed to His glorious body, according to the working by which He is able even to subdue all things to Himself" (Philippians 3:20,21).

The Church now lives in the time Jesus described in the parable of the wheat and tares as the time of harvest (Matthew 13:30). We are now in harvest time! The earth is ripe for reaping. The trumpet of God is now sounding for the Church to "thrust in the sickle" and gather the great harvest of the earth (Revelation 14:15). The next decade will be the greatest ingathering of people who comprehend the truths of God's Word that the world has ever known. We live in the day when the power of God's Word will separate the wheat and the tares (Hebrews 4:12).

The transcending Church, moving from this present age to the age to come, is discovering the reality of this transition. Jesus promised that those who leave possessions and relationships behind them in this age to follow His calling in their lives will receive rewards both now and in the age to come (Mark 10:29,30). He warned that blasphemy against the Holy Spirit is a sin which carries irrevocable penalty from this age into the age to come (Matthew 12:32). We now have a foretaste of the Kingdom of God. The writer of Hebrews warned against walking away from having tasted God's Word and the power of the age to come (Hebrews 6:5).

Two events must occur to end this present age. First, Jesus Christ will come again in power and glory (Matthew 24:30). Secondly, Satan's rule on

earth will end. World systems, Babylon, will fall
while God's people rejoice. Our mortal flesh, human
bodies that die, will put on immortality (1 Corinthians 15:54). The reign of Christ on earth will begin the
age to come. We are preparing for the rule of Christ
now when we agree with God's will daily by praying,
"Thy Kingdom come on earth as it is in heaven . . ."

We must live as Jesus did, with one foot in our
generation and the other foot planted firmly in the
age to come. This is the meaning of being "heavenly
minded" and "seeking those things which are above."
We are heavenly minded toward our earthly circumstances. Abraham understood transcending his circumstances. He would not consider the age of his
body as an obstacle to God's promise of an heir. He
believed so much in the age to come that he was willing to sacrifice Isaac, his promised child, believing
that God would raise him back to life (Genesis 22:5).

Jesus told the story of Lazarus and the rich man as
an example of rewards transcending this age (Luke
16:19-31). Lazarus was a poor beggar who was registered in the heavenlies. In fact, the angels carried
Lazarus to Abraham's bosom when he died. The rich
man, on the other hand, was sentenced to eternal
torment. These men represent the difference between
the Church and world systems. Christians must now
choose the state in which they will receive rewards.
Of course, this story is not to commend begging, nor
to oppose having riches. The principle focus of this
story is transcending one's present age into the age
to come. God's justice eternally recompenses us for
our choice of values in this present age with either
rewards or punishment.

What will the age to come be like? Jesus will be
King. That means righteousness and justice will

reign. We will know eternal peace from conflicting circumstances. Joy will continually fill our hearts. We'll live as the New Jerusalem which John described in his Revelation (Revelation 21). We'll enjoy new bodies which will be totally free from the law of sin and death. Relationships will surround us based on total and complete harmony with God and one another. The tabernacle of God will be with men in the culmination of heaven and earth, coming together to fulfill the plan of redemption (Ephesians 1:9,10).

Jesus, the "firstfruit of many brethren," took the keys of death, hell and the grave from Satan. Now the body of Christ must complete the work which Christ began. He will return for a bride who is prepared to rule with Him. The completion of Christ is the process of making us complete in Him. Completion means maturity, obedience and love. Completion means carrying out Christ's purpose of withstanding the gates of hell and destroying the works of the devil (1 John 3:8). We take ground from Satan now; then Christ returns to complete the defeat of His ancient foe.

As the body of Christ matures, we are already seeing evidences of the age to come within our generation. The Church presses toward the age to come whenever we cast out devils and heal the sick in Jesus' name. The word of faith in our mouths proclaims God's will in our circumstances. We oppose obstacles to God's will with our thoughts, words, intentions and works which bring glory to God. Tremendous strides of coming into unity among Christians today is further evidence that the age to come is very near. Love transcends doctrinal differences among Christians whose one goal is to lift up the name of Jesus.

A fresh understanding of covenant with God and the mystery of the sacraments causes the Church to transcend traditions, to come into unity with the Lord and one another. We no longer regard the sacraments of baptism, communion at the Lord's table, or tithing as symbolic, optional acts of worship. The sacramental presence of Christ is found as we activate covenant with God.

Covenant relationships are vital to our mission. The body of Christ is "fitly joined together" to accomplish God's will. Worship focuses on becoming God's pleasure. We were created to magnify and worship Him. All these are evidences, a foretaste of the age to come, assuring us by the power of the Holy Spirit that we stand on the brink of its total realization.

Paul and Silas were chained in prison at Philippi. They must have smelled the stench of the dark cell, and felt the damp, cold walls surrounding them. They had been physically beaten with rods, and then imprisoned for "exceedingly troubling the city" with their preaching of the gospel (Acts 16:20).

About midnight, one of the men suggested that they sing songs of worship and praise to the Lord. By an act of their wills, they transcended the miserable conditions of that cell to move into a realm of peace and joy in God's presence. Suddenly, the building shook. The doors to the cells opened and all the prisoners' chains fell to the floor. The eternal realm, to which Paul and Silas had moved by the Spirit, impacted with supernatural force, invading their present circumstances. The jailer [world systems] became subject to the Kingdom men he had held in bondage. He fell at their feet, trembling in fear and begging for mercy (Acts 16:19-33).

Another Kingdom man, Stephen, had preached boldly to an angry mob, infuriating them with the truth of his message. As they began to curse and shout accusations against him, he looked up into the heavens. His spirit soared into another realm. Suddenly, the heavens opened. Stephen saw the glory of God, and Jesus standing at the right hand of the Father. His face must have radiated glorious light as he proclaimed the scene spread across the sky before him. The hatred and threats against him no longer held any power.

The mob was enraged. They screamed and covered their ears at Stephen's words. They forcefully brought him back to the reality of their control, their realm of dominion. They physically dragged him out of the city and threw stones at him. But even as he was dying, bleeding and crushed, Stephen's spirit transcended the realm of historical time. He called upon the Lord, crying out, "Lord Jesus, receive my spirit!" (Acts 6 and 7).

Paul and Silas ministered to the terrified jailer, forgiving him, ministering to him and then bringing his entire household to Jesus. Stephen's dying words were for the forgiveness of his murderers. How do men transcend the present age to move toward the age to come?

Paul received heavenly visions and revelations in which he was taken into the third heaven (2 Corinthians 12:2-4). Peter received a vision of living beasts in a large sheet being lowered from the sky. God told Peter, "Rise, Peter; kill and eat." This vision symbolized the opening of the gospel of Christ to the Gentiles, which Peter would never have accepted according to Jewish traditions (Acts 11:5-10).

John received a series of revelations of Jesus

Christ recorded in his Revelation. These visions given to John impacted this age with revelations of the age to come which gave hope to Christians under grave persecution. The prophet Joel proclaimed that in the last days God would pour out His Spirit on all flesh. Spiritual visions and dreams from God would verify and give guidance in this day of preparation. Sons and daughters would prophesy.

For the sake of those Christians who are still skeptical of thousands of people claiming to have spiritual dreams and visions from God, allow me to give a practical application of this means of spiritual guidance. Moses sent twelve spies into the promised land to evaluate Israel's ability to enter the land which was then populated with hostile nations. Only two of those twelve men, Joshua and Caleb, believed Israel could enter the territory. The others brought back reports of overwhelming obstacles. The unfavorable reports of those ten men swayed the entire nation of Israel into a state of fear and unbelief. The people complained against Moses. God declared in anger that none of the spies except Joshua and Caleb would enter the land.

God said to Moses, "But My servant Caleb, because he has a different spirit in him and has followed Me fully, I will bring into the land where he went, and his descendents shall inherit it" (Numbers 14:24). Today God searches for Joshua and Caleb spirits. These men witnessed the same conditions in the land as the other spies. God said the difference in Caleb's vision, compared to the others, was his spirit of faith. He transcended the obstacles to proclaim God's will for the children of Israel. He urged Israel to put their confidence in God's strength into action. He had visions and dreams of victory for Israel, and there-

182

fore, he had no fear in fully following the Lord against powerful enemies.

Caleb exemplifies one who understands the implementation and the benefits of covenant with God. The blood covenant of circumcision given to Abraham and then Israel has its counterpart in New Testament water baptism. The blood covenant for a Christian is established through the blood of Jesus Christ shed on the cross. In baptism, the believer dies to his old nature to be resurrected with Christ to newness of life. To be in covenant with God means that our confidence is in the Lord and in the power of His might.

We celebrate that life in communion at the Lord's table. The historical debate among Christians on transubstantiation of the bread and the fruit of the vine (juice or wine) will possibly not be resolved with certainty until the Lord comes. However, I do believe that Jesus meant the exact wording He used when He said, "This is My body . . . This is My blood . . ."

The Church is only beginning to comprehend the significance of the sacraments as being more than symbolic adherence to Church traditions. Covenant with God is essential to accomplish His will in the earth. "Sacrament" means "mystery." Paul compared the mystery of Christ and the Church to the marriage relationship between a man and his wife in which two become one. The full meaning of covenant with God holds mysteries beyond our comprehension. The mysteries of God recorded in His Word are unfolding to the generation that comprehends God's intention to fill the earth with His glory through the witness of His covenant people. Otherwise, Paul would never have told the Church to pray for the spirit of wisdom and revelation in the knowledge of

Christ (Ephesians 1:16,17).

So what does covenant have to do with dreams and visions? Covenant is established by our willingness to obey God. Spiritual dreams and visions are given by the Holy Spirit to those who are seeking first the Kingdom of God and His righteousness. How extensive and frequent are genuine spiritual dreams and visions among God's people? I doubt that anyone is qualified to answer that question. We are told by both Joel and Peter (who quotes the prophet Joel in his sermon on the Day of Pentecost) that the Holy Spirit is poured out on all flesh.

God's Word clearly indicates that without a vision the people perish. As I have stated previously, the New Testament indicates that spiritual leaders are often given visions from God. When someone shares a vision or dream that is truly given by the Lord, the Holy Spirit quickens confirmation within the hearts of covenant people—those who have Caleb spirits.

Please let me emphasize that spiritual visions and dreams always, without exception, must be in keeping with God's recorded Word and the character of Jesus Christ. Likewise, visions and dreams must always be submitted to spiritual eldership in the body of Christ—either verbally through counsel, or by spiritual leaders' confirmation of direction as God begins to open circumstances to bring about the fulfillment of that which He has ordained. The final test of spiritual visions and dreams is the fruit they yield. Does the fruit honor the Lord? Does it bring glory to God or feed someone's ego? Does it draw people to Jesus Christ and bring abundant life to them? Reflect on the spiritual fruit of Paul's or John's life. They endured tremendous persecution for the sake of the gospel of Jesus Christ. Yet, Paul confidently

184

stood before King Agrippa saying, "I was not disobedient to the heavenly vision . . ." (Acts 26:19).

Covenant with God calls for a demonstration of responsible Christianity. Covenant Christians are involved in their communities to insure opportunities for abundant life. They care about political, ecological and social issues which threaten freedom and creativity among people. Responsible Christianity demands that love becomes a primary motive for action. Love always restores. Love covers a multitude of sins. Christ's love within us is the most powerful force on earth against oppression. Speaking the truth in love always brings people to freedom.

Secondly, covenant Christians demonstrate responsible Christianity by sharing their inheritance. God has always made provisions for His people. He promised an eternal inheritance to Abraham's seed— Israel, then Jesus Christ, and now the Church. In Jewish culture, the oldest son received a double portion of the inheritance. He alone had the authority to free slaves or annul debts owed to his family. The Scripture tells us that Jesus is the firstborn of many brethren. Since He is the elder brother, we can understand the meaning of the scripture which says, ". . . if the Son makes you free, you shall be free indeed . . ." (John 8:36).

Covenant Christians demonstrate responsible Christianity when they learn how to complete their brothers and sisters in Christ. How can God judge strife in the world when competition and mistrust dominate ministries? How can God judge jealousy in the world when Christians resent the blessings of others? The Church is no demonstration to the world when Christians are impoverished in one nation, and live lavishly in another. Ministries whom God has blessed

185

with resources and provisions must regard themselves as storehouses for ministries in need. Perhaps this is one of the greatest tests for maturity and unity in the bride of Christ.

Future Trends

Until Christ reigns in heaven and earth as King of kings and Lord of lords, the Church is challenged to wage war against all forces opposing God's plan. Allow me to prophesy seven areas of conflict which will war against our unity of faith in the next decade. Remember that the central message of this book has been an answer to Jesus' prayer in John 17, ". . . that they [the Church] may be one . . . that the world may believe . . ."

1. Christians will begin to shine in the marketplaces of society. God will grant solutions through the Church to answer major social, medical, technological and political problems. The same recognition as He gave to Joseph and Daniel will manifest His glory throughout the earth through His covenant people. Simultaneously, distinct battlelines will be drawn between the "sacred" and the "secular." Humanism as a religion will become more obvious in conflicts which call biblical morality into question. Secular society will use education and government to champion their causes against the Church. Major spokesmen in those fields will clash continuously in debates with Church leaders.

2. Social concerns against the Church will focus on a "me-ism" at the expense of the welfare of the majority of people in a nation. The mind of reason will argue for "individual rights" against the good of all. Civil government will pledge to support the individual offense instead of the wishes of the majority.

As a result, proposed legislation will attempt to silence the voice of the Church as being an offensive influence in society.

3. Racial prejudice will surface in new and subtle ways. People will argue about the preservation of their ethnic identities. Christians will continue to be torn in debates concerning traditions and cultural heritage. Forms of worship in music and the arts will be one area of focus in this tug-of-war.

4. Terrorist fear tactics will become a common threat in people's lives around the world. Lawlessness will become a dominant, personal matter for people throughout the social strata. Fear will abound. People will take risks to go to shopping centers, airports, high-rises, etc. This wave of fear will teach God's people the implementation of Jesus' promise that we would "walk on serpents and scorpions." We will then learn the truth of Psalm 91 by "dwelling under the shadow of the Almighty."

5. The true Church will be attacked by religious systems according to the description in God's Word concerning signs of the end times (Matthew 24). Deceived, religious people will attack the true Church and believe that they are serving God. These people will use "white" swords and carry Bibles.

Meanwhile, the true Church will be led by the Holy Spirit at a dimension never known before. We will see battles between true revelation and pseudo-revelation; true visions and false visions; signs and wonders and lying signs and wonders. Individuals will arise with "messianic" powers of deception. Many will refuse to understand the necessity of team ministry and body life of the Church or the safety in the counsel of eldership.

While the true Church grows in intercession and a

"Samuel" advisory role to the nations, religious systems will conform to the status quo. They will have
form without power and "sit in Moses' seat" to judge
others. Many crying "orthodoxy" the loudest will
have departed from Christ's commission to His disciples recorded in Scripture.

6. The Church will continue to stand in opposition
to political ideologies such as Marxism, moralistic
opposition from the media and humanistic instruction found primarily in higher education. People in
covenant with God will be pressed into unity of faith,
or they will die in separation from one another.

7. Christians will learn to live in what I call "the
seventh dimension" in which they will, "having done
all, stand" as God intervenes in their behalf. This
"seventh dimension" is confirmation through miracles, signs and wonders. The "seventh dimension" is
the Elijah ministry amid confrontations. The focus of
ministry in the Church will move from individuals to
the ministry of the body of Christ. Healing and restoration gifts will be ministered corporately rather
than individually.

Covenant Christians demonstrate responsible Christianity whenever we activate both vertical and horizontal dimensions of our relationship with the Lord
in our lives. Daily we must seek, pray, listen and do
the will of our Father in heaven. We must also boldly
press forward toward the age to come. We will definitely meet confrontations and opposition to our
efforts, but we will never be defeated. Some will be
imprisoned for their faith; some will even face death
for their testimony to Christ. But the blood covenant
of Jesus Christ will prevail. The blood of the martyrs
cries out from the earth. The blood of Christ cries out
in behalf of the Church. Saints under the altar cry

out to God, "How long, how long, how long?" And Caleb spirits around the world respond to the cry of God's heart by rising up, shaking themselves and sounding an alarm in Zion! "Not by might, nor by power, but by His Spirit, we are more than conquerors!"

We conquer by loving one another as He loves us. We conquer by determining in our hearts to follow the leading of His Spirit. As Christ and the Father are one, we must become one with each other by the seal of the Holy Spirit within us. Together, we arise and shine His light—so the world may know . . .

ABOUT THE AUTHOR

Bishop Earl Paulk is senior pastor of Chapel Hill Harvester Church located in Atlanta, Georgia. Chapel Hill Harvester Church has twenty full-time pastors serving a local parish of over ten thousand people with thousands more receiving ministry through television and outreach ministries.

Bishop Paulk grew up in a classical Pentecostal family as the son of Earl P. Paulk Sr., a former assistant general overseer of the Church of God. His grandfather, Elisha Paulk, was a Freewill Baptist preacher.

Personal and educational exposure have given Bishop Paulk an ecumenical understanding enjoyed by few church leaders in the world today. He earned a Bachelor of Arts degree from Furman University which is a Baptist institution and a Master of Divinity degree from Candler School of Theology which is a Methodist seminary.

Earl Paulk was named to the office of Bishop in the International Communion of Charismatic Churches in 1982. He assumes oversight of many churches, directly and indirectly influenced by the ministry of Chapel Hill Harvester Church. The church hosts an annual Pastors' Conference in which leaders from local churches across the nation absorb anointed teaching, observe ministry demonstration and have the opportunity for personal dialogue on the major concerns confronting the Church today.

Under Bishop Paulk's leadership, Chapel Hill Harvester Church has become a successful working prototype of a true Kingdom Church. The foundation of the church is Kingdom principles applied to the biblical concept of a City of Refuge.

The church ministries include a home for unwed mothers; a licensed child placement agency; ministry to those chemically addicted and their families; a ministry to those wishing to come out of the homosexual community; outreach programs to nursing homes, prisons, and homebound individuals; Alpha, one of the most widely acclaimed youth ministries in the nation; and many other ministries designed to meet the needs of the Body of Christ.

Television outreach through the Harvester Television Network is the "Earl Paulk" program seen weekly on P.T.L. Satellite Network, Trinity Broadcasting Network, Rock Network and numerous other television outlets nationwide. Bishop Paulk is frequently a guest on major television and radio interview programs, discussing his books and issues which focus on the Kingdom message.

Other books by K-Dimension Publishers

The Divine Runner   Earl Paulk

Ultimate Kingdom   Earl Paulk

The Wounded Body of Christ   Earl Paulk

Satan Unmasked   Earl Paulk

Sex Is God's Idea   Earl Paulk

Held In The Heavens Until . . .   Earl Paulk

Thrust In The Sickle and Reap   Earl Paulk

To Whom Is God Betrothed?   Earl Paulk

The Provoker (The biography of Earl Paulk)   Tricia Weeks

My All-Sufficient One   Sharon Price

For further information please contact:

P.O. Box 7300 • Atlanta, GA 30357

For further information please call:

Compassion Publishers

Chapel Hill Harvester Church publishes a monthly newsletter, *Thy Kingdom Come,* which is available by subscription for $10.00 per year.

If you would like to subscribe to *Thy Kingdom Come,* send the following form or a facsimile, along with your payment to:

Chapel Hill Harvester Church
Thy Kingdom Come
P.O. Box 371289
Decatur, Georgia 30037

— — — — — — — — — — — — — — — — —

I would like to subscribe to your monthly newsletter, *Thy Kingdom Come.* Enclosed is my payment of $10.00.

Name _____

Address _____

City _____ State _____

Zip Code _____ Phone (_____)_____